The Roots Grow Deep

A story of Captain Ford, his son Edward and their contribution to America's glass industry . . . . and a picture of people and events that helped to build our land.

Sponsored by

LIBBEY · OWENS · FORD GLASS COMPANY

Research and Writing by

WILLIAM EARL AIKEN

Privately Printed Edition

Published by The Lezius-Hiles Company · Cleveland, Ohio

1957

CHAPTER INDEX

See page 89 for detailed index of personalities, companies and places.

EDWARD FORD
1843-1920

The Magic That Is America

It began as a trickle.

Eight Dutch and Polish glass blowers, members of Capt. John Smith's English colonizing expedition, built a crude furnace on an island in the James River in 1608—America's first industrial enterprise.

The trickle became a rivulet, then a brook; and the brook became a river. The river crested, flooding the land . . . children from the Old World grew up in the New World.

Their children's children populated the hills and the prairies, their labors and their inventions brought factories, shops, schools, hospitals and homes—sometimes to encompass a lone farm house.

Their ideals, their sweat and their blood, their sorrows and their triumphs, their births and their deaths, their indomitable courage— pooled in the magic that is America.

They are the dead and the living . . . the people who made and are making . . .

"A Great Name In Glass"

CHAPTER 1

In the Beginning

The roots of Rossford grow deep.

Although youngest community in the valley of the Maumee, perhaps in all of Ohio, Rossford dates its ancestry back to those days when guns of a British fleet ruled near-by Lake Erie.

Those familiar with its background know that Rossford was founded in 1898 by a distinguished plate glass manufacturer, Edward Ford, and that the community's name is a combination of Mr. Ford's name and the maiden name of his wife, Caroline J. Ross.

Few, however, know that Rossford would never have been born as such had it not been for a Kentuckian, John B. Ford—father of Edward Ford.

What Edward Ford brought to Rossford and what he accomplished there can best be understood by turning the spotlight for a moment upon one of America's truly great pioneer industrialists, the "Father of the American Plate Glass Industry."

John Baptiste Ford was born in a log cabin in the wilderness settlement of Danville, Kentucky, in 1811—a few years before Commodore Perry defeated a British fleet on Lake Erie. And as this tiny infant lay in his log cradle, fate placed an invisible mark on his red little forehead, a mark that destined this wilderness child to sire a son who would found Rossford 87 long years later—close by Commodore Perry's victory far to the north.

John was the third child of Jonathan and Margaret Ford. Margaret was the daughter of Jean Baptiste, who had come from France and fought in the American Revolution. After the war he had joined the westward migration, following the Wilderness Trail from Virginia through Cumberland Gap into the Dark and Bloody Ground that was to become Kentucky.

He settled upon his government-awarded 300 acres just outside the cluster of cabins and stockade known as Danville. It was there that his youngest daughter, Margaret, married Jonathan Ford when she was a scant 15 years old.

Little is known of Jonathan, except that he was from Virginia and believed to have been of English descent. Despite this, he seems to have borne a hatred for the British, inasmuch as he left his family to enlist in a Kentucky Volunteer Homespun regiment that marched away late in 1813 to fight the British in New Orleans.

Mrs. Ford was only 22 at this time, carrying her fourth child. Jonathan was never heard of again, so young John couldn't even remember his father.

When John was about 12, Mrs. Ford apprenticed him to a Danville saddlemaker on his promise that he would teach her son to read and write.

Two years later, in 1825, John ran away—grief stricken over the death of his beloved grandfather, Jean Baptiste, and angered by the saddlemaker's failure to keep his pomise.

John's runaway was no childish lark, dreamed up on the spur of the moment. Aware that rewards were posted for runaway apprentices, he knew he must avoid the known roads, lonely as they were. There were only two—the more traveled one northward to Lexington, the other westward and north to Bardstown.

He wanted to get to Louisville. In his limited knowledge of the country, it represented the farthest possible distance he could go . . . he knew, too, that once he reached Louisville, there was a river. If he could get across, it meant freedom—safety from capture.

One warm morning, long before dawn, he slipped away, disappearing into the vast forest. As he slowly progressed, it became a terrifying experience . . . the eerie silence by day, when only an occasional shaft of sunlight penetrated the deep gloom at high noon . . . the menacing sounds at night, the sudden snap of a twig, the hair-raising rustle of something nearby.

His clothing ripped, his feet and hands cruelly cut as he fought against the seemingly impenetrable tangle of never-ending wild growth that clutched and pulled

against his every step, this 14-year-old boy revealed the astonishing determination and courage that was to characterize his whole life.

Many days and nights later, John Ford finally saw Louisville in the distance. The strange sights fascinated and confused him, but he kept on—heading for that river. And as he slipped along the streets, moving in and out among the plodding teams of oxen as they strained with their loads, weaving from side to side as their cursing drivers maneuvered past the tree stumps in the streets, John presented a strange spectacle, even in these rugged surroundings.

No living man, seeing this half-starved boy, limping along painfully, with the furtiveness of a hunted animal,

Ford's father-in-law and mother-in-law

could know that some day a statue would be unveiled in his honor.

Courage that knew no limits and an iron will took John Ford to the river. And still another trait that was to mark his entire life enabled him to cross that river— The Ohio.

He had no money to pay for his passage on the crude little ferry, but he traded one of his few possessions, a deck of playing cards, to the riverman. Call it salesmanship or promotional ability, John got aboard.

He wasn't exactly a paying passenger. The ferryman, despite the angry protests of a woman passenger, insisted upon the boy climbing into a small pen at one end of the ferry and standing among the pigs being shipped to New Albany.

John didn't mind at all. His eyes were glued upon freedom as the Indiana shore approached. . . . Up on the bluff after landing at New Albany, a town only six years older than himself, John Ford looked back across the Ohio. The Kentucky shore looked too close for his comfort. Once more he faded into the woods, stopping only after he had reached the settlement of Greenville, up in the timbered hills 12 miles northwest of New Albany.

Here he would remain for 30 years—three eventful and fruitful decades, but diluted with bitter tragedy.

Becoming a saddler's apprentice again when he arrived in Greenville, young Ford eventually bought the shop. His restless urge led him into operating a small grocery and dry goods store. Unable to read or write, he soon found himself in difficulties. At the end of a week he couldn't determine who owed him or how much.

Ford solved that problem by falling in love and marrying Mary Bower, a farm girl who taught him to read and write. That was in 1831, when he was 20. Young Ford began to prosper, yet the pattern of his material success became lined with threads of domestic sorrows.

The young couple's first child, Charles, died within nine months of its birth. John, second child, died at 10 months. Henry Ford, third child, died when he was 15 years old. Meantime, their first girl baby, born two years after Henry, died at the age of eight.

John Ford's mother, Margaret, who had come from Danville about 1837 to Greenville, died in August of 1840. Ford's fifth child, Mary, died four months later, two days before Christmas—living only five days!

In the first nine years of his married life, Ford had lost four of five children and his mother, who had died at 48. And John Ford still was only 29 years old.

Home of Ford and bride in Greenville. Clapboard added years later.

Flour mill operated by young Ford in Greenville

Larger home occupied by Ford family. Originally of log construction.

Adversity, however, had a rough time trying to ride the broad shoulders of this young man. He expanded his saddlery shop. He operated a flour mill. And before long he was to have more than 30 teams on the road, his agents selling perforated tin cabinets, known as "kitchen safes," to farm wives, and saddles and harness for the men folk.

The Mexican War gave Ford his first big break. Winning a contract to supply saddles and harness to units of the United States Cavalry, he made enough money to influence him to try the one thing that had been in his mind for years . . . he wanted to make things.

He had proven himself a leader, one who could handle men; and his advice had been sought by older men. His great energy demanded more than this frontier community could provide. His urge to make things seemed coupled to his amazing ability to see future needs by analyzing current conditions and methods.

The vast country west of the Mississippi was still a land of marauding savages and adventurers, but in his own lifetime Ford had seen transportation beginning to improve—the bellowing sternwheel steamers (only four years older than himself) replacing the graceful keel boat and the crude raft on the Ohio; he himself had helped to build a part of the plank road between New Albany, Paoli and St. Louis where it passed through Greenville; and by now Fort Dearborn, bogged in the eternal prairie mud on the shore of Lake Michigan, had become the town of Chicago.

Pine knot torches and candles were still the means of illumination as John Ford sold all his Greenville business enterprises, and moved into New Albany in 1854 with his wife and two small sons, Edward and Emory. By the standard of the times, Ford was a wealthy man. He had $40,000 in the bank.

What an incredible contrast, his return to New Albany and that day 29 years before when he first walked along High street, his clothes in shreds, his feet bleeding, his only possessions an awl and a knife.

If the three decades he had just passed would make an absorbing book, the next two were to be even more fascinating—for John, for New Albany, for Indiana and for all the 31 states of the nation.

Ford's first manufacturing venture as a citizen of New Albany was the production of a feed cutting box for farmers, a simple affair of wood and iron, with a manually operated cutting blade, patterned after a Sanford cutter for which he had purchased the rights for four states.

Expanding his operations, he started a small nail factory. His dislike of purchasing anything he could make, led him into a partnership in an iron rolling mill. Later he developed this into a large operation, the Ohio Falls and New Albany Rolling Mills. That was followed by a forge works and a foundry, and the manufacture of plows.

All this took place in a matter of two or three years. And while his operations made money, due in great part to the opening up of the West, Ford early sensed that Pittsburgh and other up-river communities were rapidly

New Albany of old. At right, Ohio river. Note manufacturing buildings, foundries, etc., where Ford operated. From an old lithograph.

The St. James, a Ford-built packet. From Capt.
Fred Way, Jr.'s collection.

Ford-built twin stacker for Red River operation.
Fred Way, Jr. collection.

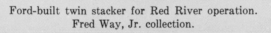

Another Ford-built fast packet, the
Wild Wagoner . . . Courtesy Fred
Way, Jr.

Part of Ford shipyard

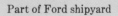

taking over a dominating position in iron and steel.

By now the steamboat had become the great common carrier, handling vast tonnage, a fact that Ford began to contemplate carefully. Analyzing his own river-front enterprises, he discovered that the bulk of his iron mill, foundry and forge products were being taken by local shipbuilders and some of the larger ones across the river at Louisville.

That was a challenge, and almost before anyone realized it, John Ford was in the shipbuilding business. Not only did he build and sell steamboats, but he operated the bigger ones and soon there was the Ford fleet of carriers and fast dispatch boats.

By 1859, five years after he had arrived in New Albany, John B. Ford had a very sizable boat works and river fleet, and the inevitable happened. He came to be known as Captain Ford, a title that was to cling throughout his life.

And now, just as the Mexican War had given him a great opportunity to sell saddles when he was in Greenville, the Civil War provided an even greater opportunity. The Union forces took every ship Ford could muster as troop carriers. At the siege of Vicksburg, General Grant for a time used a shell-scarred Ford boat for his personal transportation.

In his early fifties, Capt. Ford worked night and day in the interests of the Union cause, and one of his many enterprises, some quite daring in conception, merits recording here. Before the Monitor and Merrimac officially ended marine warfare in wooden boats forever, Capt. Ford had already helped to set the stage for it.

Ford boats, returning from downriver encounters on the Mississippi, limped into the Ford boatyard, ripped and torn by cannon fire. Capt. Ford worked his crews through the nights—covering his ships with great sheets of iron.

The start of the war had throttled lucrative river trade to and from New Orleans, but had given Ford an opportunity to sell transportation to the military.

Business continued to flourish for a time, but Capt. Ford's keen mind once more sensed a change coming. He had retained his iron interests, but only that he could be in a better position to build his ships. He had intended that his fleet would be one of the largest on the Ohio, but he canceled his greatest shipbuilding enterprise, the construction of 12 new majestic Twin Stack steamers, each to be named for one of the Apostles, when he became convinced that the rush to develop railroads after the Civil War would make great inroads on Ohio river traffic.

Ford began to look around for a new business venture, even as he continued his many activities along the New Albany river front. The opportunity came through one of his sons, Emory.

Emory was graduated from Merchants College in Pittsburgh in June of 1864. Just 18, he returned to New Albany to find a niche in the business life of the community. He recounted to a friend his enthusiasm for glass, explaining that he had often visited one or another of the numerous glass plants at Pittsburgh to watch the glass-blowers at their picturesque trade.

Word of Emory's enthusiasm reached Capt. Ford, who

Capt. Ford in 1864

Mrs. Ford (Mary Bower) in 1864

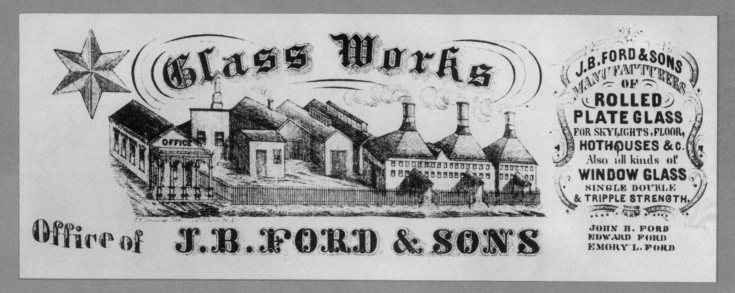

Ford's first glass factory on New Albany river bank

had long been anxious for his sons to manifest their interest in manufacturing.

Capt. Ford bought additional ground along the water front and soon another new industry for New Albany budded—J. B. Ford & Sons, manufacturers of bottles and fruit jars. (A small window glass plant was added later.)

The icy winds of financial troubles to come began to blow across the land. For Capt. Ford these winds became bitter blasts, and they were particularly difficult for this optimistic, jovial and hard-driving man who believed in people to the point where he became careless in signing notes for acquaintances and business associates.

His wealth estimated at well above $300,000 in solid and tangible assets at the peak of the Civil War period, Capt. Ford now found himself in a cascading avalanche. Not only had business for his rolling mills, foundry and forge works dropped sharply, but his fleet of 28 boats was at wharf-side much of the time.

He hung on grimly, selling some of his boats, mostly at losses, to meet his more pressing obligations. Other business ventures up and down the New Albany waterfront, in which he had stock, began to fail. Large sums he had loaned to business associates and friends were never paid back to him.

Capt. Ford moved his desk from his water-front office to the small glass works, the one business that seemed to continue to hold promise of a profit. He would sell glass instead of transportation. But his two sons in charge were faced with problems, too, in this picturesque but strange and tricky operation. Capt. Ford took what cash he had to meet payrolls, but the pressure continued and the contractors who had built the little plant took it over.

While it was in their possession, the small glass works burned down. Rebuilding it and not caring to get involved in a business they did not understand, the con-

One of Ford's first glass advertisements

tractors traded it back to Capt. Ford for one of his steamers.

No one could ever fathom Mr. Ford's nimble mind, except to be amazed by his incredible ability to swing from one enterprise to another with surprising suddenness, usually at a quick profit. Now nearing 60, Capt. Ford might well be expected to sit tight, wait until his assets could be liquidated, and retire, letting his two sons fight their own problems with the little glass plant.

But Capt. Ford wasn't put together that way. When he left his steamboat office for the glass works, he apparently had made up his mind, without telling even his own sons, that he was ready for another fight.

What a battle it turned out to be—the greatest of his career, and his most successful, but not before he was mauled and bruised, literally beaten to the ground before he could struggle to his feet again.

With the rebuilt plant back in the family again, Capt. Ford gave all his attention to the manufacture of glass. Gambling most of his available cash, he bought two more blocks along the water-front and erected expensive buildings. This expanded operation became famous as the New Albany Glass Works. (Later this plant changed names and ownership several times.)

Ford's expansion was not due to any desire to enlarge his window glass and bottle production. He well knew that there was enormous competition in these fields. He had discovered that plate glass was not produced in this country, that all polished plate came from Europe.

This fired his imagination. Why wasn't it being produced in America?

Systematically, he asked every glass employee in the plant. They were either window glass or bottle blowers. They couldn't give him a satisfactory answer. He read every article on glass he could find. Finally, he wrote a letter to Scientific American magazine about it. The editor's reply pointed out that America had no equipment or facilities to produce it, no glass technicians who knew how to make such glass.

It seemed logical to give up the plan. But Capt. Ford bored in. He learned the name of a young English plate glass grinder who wanted to come to America. Capt. Ford sent for him—John Cooper, who was to remain with Ford throughout his life. Cooper's son-in-law, Matthias R. Pepper, wanted to come over from England, too. He was an expert polisher in one of the big plate glass plants. With their help, Ford imported the first plate glass equipment ever brought to America.

Cooper, the grinder, and Pepper, the polisher, were soon followed by other eager Englishmen and a trickle of Scotsmen, Belgians, Frenchmen and Germans—all young plate glass men eager to try for a place in the raw new world.

This small group of foreign-born helped Capt. Ford to write a new declaration of industrial independence for America. And it was a proud moment indeed as Capt. Ford watched his men install the first two panes of polished plate glass ever made in America in the store front of John Heib's tailor shop at 318 Pearl street in New Albany.

(The store front is still there, although housing another business now. Many years after their installation, the historic panes were removed to the homes of two of Capt. Ford's granddaughters, Mrs. Nell Ford Torrey and Mrs. Stella Ford Schlotman of Detroit.)

First installation of Ford-made polished plate glass

Original panes installed in New Albany store front purchased many years ago, mirrored and placed in home of a Ford granddaughter, Mrs. Harry N. Torrey, Detroit, nee Nellie Blanche Ford, daughter of Emory Ford, brother of Edward Ford.

Capt. Ford had proved that plate glass could be made in America. He had proved, too, that his products were good. The Indiana State Board of Agriculture awarded two medals for exhibits of his glass, one for polished plate glass in 1871 to a distributor, Hannaman & Company, the other with this legend: "Awarded to J. B. Ford, New Albany, Indiana, Collection of Window Glass, Indiana Manufacture, 1872."

But medal-winning products do not necessarily mean ready sales, and Capt. Ford found this to be true even in those days.

He thought of his market in terms of the countless store windows, mirrors and show cases of merchants in the cities and towns and small communities within a hundred or so miles. Surely they would want the fine glass he was now making.

He had faith in Americans wanting American-made products. But glass distributors, well-stocked with the better known and long-accepted French plate, and the plate glass of England and Germany, were slow to respond. And this pioneering American manufacturer had no protective tariff to aid him, a fact that enabled the well-entrenched European manufacturers to flood the American shores with glass by lowering their prices to such an extent that it could be sold at retail for less per square foot than Capt. Ford could make it.

Ford sold everything he had in a desperate attempt to keep his small plant going full steam ahead, refusing to lay off workers and doggedly visiting Louisville, Cincinnati and other markets in an effort to sell his plate glass.

At a time when he was awarded medals for the excellency of his products, Capt. Ford was forced to the wall. His plant was taken over by his biggest stockholder, his own cousin, Washington C. DePauw, at that time one of Indiana's wealthiest men—banker and grain baron, a man with vast holdings in western mines, and a force behind the scenes in Indiana politics.

Clawed clean of everything except his great courage

Letterhead of Louisville Plate Glass Company. Note John B. Ford listed as superintendent.

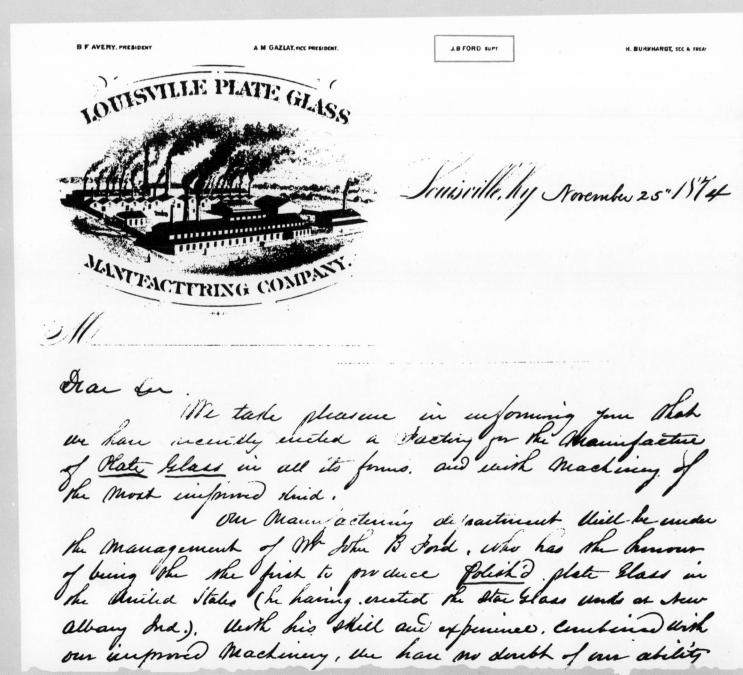

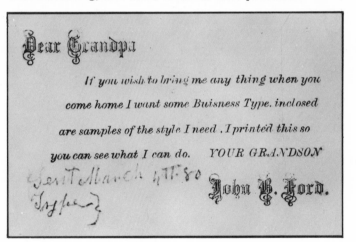

and indomitable will, Capt. Ford crossed the river to Louisville, where in 1874, he supervised the construction of a plant much larger than the one in New Albany. He accepted the superintendency of the new works, the Louisville Plate Glass Company. One year later he walked out, when he discovered that his name had been used by the promoters in immensely over-capitalizing it on paper and under-manning it physically with technically skilled men.

Capt. Ford re-crossed the river, constructing a small plant in Jeffersonville, a few miles upriver from New Albany. His two sons rejoined him.

That was in 1877, the black panic still upon the land. Poor equipment, most of it second hand, and meager funds were the handicaps; loyal employees who had followed Ford from New Albany to Louisville and back to Jeffersonville the inadequate assets.

The philosophy of mass production was still an unheralded dogma of American industry of the 1870's, but Capt. Ford sensed its essentials when he ventured into the glass business. That's what led him hopefully to Louisville, and now at Jeffersonville he soon realized that the only way to establish American plate glass manufacture on a profitable basis was to build larger and larger plants, and win the fight for a protective tariff. That required huge capital.

That he was 69 years old and broke when he decided to try again, and succeeded, is one of the unsung sagas of American industry, never fully understood except by the few who knew the details.

Capt. Ford had been as quick to seek a bank loan as he had been to loan money to a needy acquaintance, but now—having asked for no mercy from his creditors or the bankruptcy courts—the penniless old Captain faced the toughest problem of his life. How could he raise sufficient funds to try a comeback in some other part of the country?

The answer came from an unexpected source, a former employee, George A. Schmitt, who had hauled glass for Mr. Ford for years. The German-born teamster, whose goose-neck wagon and little bay mare had hauled that first historic load of plate glass from the Ford factory to Mr. Heib's store front, took $100 from his savings and handed it to Capt. Ford.

Many men in a similar position might well have spurned such an offer, but not the old Captain. He accepted it gladly, not only because it solved his problem for the moment, but because, as he often said

years later, it proved his life-long attitude toward labor—maintenance of respect and equality of employer and employee for each other.

George Schmitt's loan was, in many ways, the most important Capt. Ford ever received. It enabled him to depart for new scenes—but with little else in his possession except a reputation for unimpeachable honesty, a keen knowledge of human nature, a wide experience in manufacturing, and some ideas for new products.

Dear Grandpa

If you wish to bring me any thing when you come home I want some Buisness Type. inclosed are samples of the style I need . I printed this so you can see what I can do. YOUR GRANDSON

John B. Ford.

Like his grandpa, John B. Ford, named for the Old Captain, and son of Edward, early showed promotional ability by typing a note to Capt. Ford after the latter had left for the East. It was typed in March, 1880.

Leaving The Valley was not easy. Here were the scenes of his childhood, his rise to fame and wealth, hundreds upon hundreds of friends and acquaintances. Here was his aging wife, tight-lipped and ill. Here were Edward and Emory, working long days and worrying through long nights in the hopeless struggle to make plate glass at a profit. . . . Emory, still in his early 30's, with a wife and infant daughter; Edward, with four children, the youngest less than a year old. Buying provisions for the table now was a real problem for the Fords.

George Schmitt, who had hauled glass for Capt. Ford at New Albany, loaned $100 to Mr. Ford to help him leave for the East to try a comeback.

A Fighting Face. Taken in that era when the Old Captain was fighting for money and a higher tariff in his stirring Comeback days.

No wonder the Old Captain turned away so quickly as he kissed his wife good-bye. He waited until he had turned the corner before he stopped, took off his glasses and wiped his eyes. Then he walked on, chin thrust forward. The Old Lion was on the prowl again.

His goal was New York City, but first he stopped in Pittsburgh, where acquaintances of his steamboat days resided. Using the iron and steel metropolis, where the clanging throb of industry was music to his heart, as his base of operations, Capt. Ford pulled the throttle of his boundless energy wide open.

In New York, he won an audience with Peter Cooper, the aged philanthropist and inventor. This in itself was a tribute to Capt. Ford. Men were hired to do nothing but keep away the endless chain of people, who made Peter Cooper's door the mecca for worthy charities and crack-pot ideas.

The elderly inventor, now nearing 90, liked Capt. Ford's idea—glass sewer pipe.

The Old Captain, who had properly patented his idea, had a cumbersome but interesting sample of glass sewer pipe with him.

Peter Cooper's son-in-law, Abram S. Hewitt, then mayor of New York, was faced with the problem of improving and greatly extending the rapidly-growing city's sewer system.

Peter Cooper was instrumental in having Ford's patent rights bought for $17,000. The plan for sewer pipe never materialized, but Ford had much-needed cash in hand—enough to send a good sum back to Jeffersonville, and to continue his search for sufficient funds to start a plant and to continue his campaign for an adequate protective tariff on plate glass.

His resourcefulness was as limitless as his energy. Two episodes will serve to illustrate. During a visit in Boston, he learned that large tracts in Massachusetts, worthless for farming, could be bought very cheaply. Visiting some of the sandy stretches of worthless acreage, he detected glass sand. He bought a large tract. With his reputation as a glassmaker to back him, Capt. Ford re-sold at a quick profit.

His keen interest in human nature led him to another profitable enterprise. If he saw a man whom he didn't

Glass sewer pipe being demonstrated by Capt. Ford to famous Peter Cooper, famous inventor and philanthropist, when "JB" was fighting for funds to stage his comeback.

know, but who aroused his interest, Capt. Ford would introduce himself, and usually he found out all about the man in a short time.

On a train to New York, Mr. Ford saw a gentleman whose distinctive bearing challenged his curiosity. He proceeded to get acquainted. The man turned out to be General John C. Fremont, one of the U.S. Government's greatest pathfinders of the Western frontiers.

Obviously impressed by the distinguished Old Lion in his high silk hat and frock coat, General Fremont recounted how, 30 years before, he had acquired large Spanish grants of California land when sovereignty rights were transferred to the United States by Mexico. Years of litigation had left him land poor, and now, with titles cleared and hard pressed for cash, he was anxious to sell some of his holdings.

Before the train reached New York, Capt. Ford had made a deal. He would sell the land for the General, even though the Old Captain had never seen the properties. Tongue in cheek, the General smilingly had given his consent.

Capt. Ford earned $20,000 in commissions!

Such funds, welcome as they were, had to be used for living and traveling expenses, and to help out the folk back in Jeffersonville. If he were to build a new glass plant, he would have to have a large sum, and all in one hunk, for that specific purpose.

He finally won a hearing with two New York capitalists. Capt. Ford got the money, and hurried back to Pittsburgh.

He bought the Peterson farm at Hite's Station, a whistle-stop on the old West Penn railroad, later named Creighton, on the banks of the Allegheny river, 20 miles north of Pittsburgh.

It was not a hasty purchase. Capt. Ford already had visited the area, and he had explained the abundant and varied advantages for plate glass manufacture existing there to the New York capitalists.

With one lump sum obtained from the New York bankers, added to what he had been able to save from his previous windfalls, Capt. Ford decided to plunge. Construction began.

Bankers and other financial men of Pittsburgh who were hesitant about investing with Capt. Ford earlier, now began to buy—Capt. Ford having issued common stock in the amount of $100,000 for working capital as soon as his new company had been organized.

Now they were "with" the Old Captain

Capt. Ford's historic comeback began as he neared his 71st birthday. Ground was broken for Plant No. 1, on April 1, 1882.

The Old Lion really had his tail up now. He was here, there—everywhere at once, it seemed. He sent for Edward and for others in Jeffersonville and New Albany,

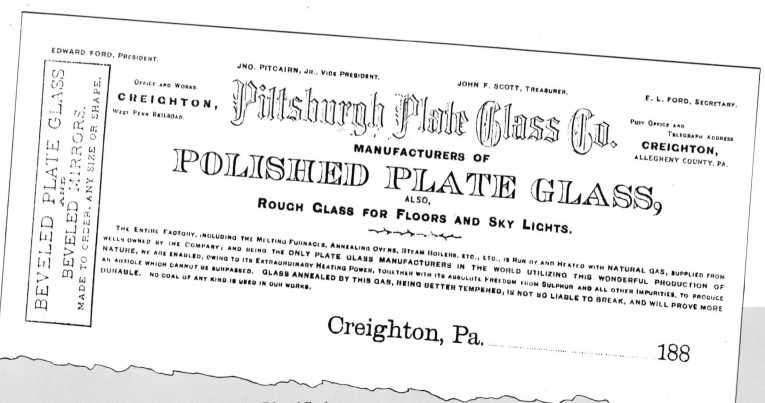

Early letterhead of Pittsburgh Plate, when Edward Ford was president and his brother Emory was secretary

where Cousin Wash DePauw's plate glass plant was foundering.

Excited families loaded their furniture into railroad boxcars as glass men, eager to join their beloved Old Captain again, began to trickle out of the Valley of the Ohio eastward to the Valley of the Allegheny—the new Promised Land for plate glass.

That it would be just that—the first real stronghold against the crippling invasions of the vast European manufacturing operations—is interestingly reflected in an article printed in a glass trade publication back in 1923—20 years after Capt. Ford's death. It said in part:

"Up to 1880, not a piece of plate glass had been made in the United States without loss to the manufacturer; all money invested had vanished without result.

"But suddenly, in the early eighties, the situation showed a remarkable change. By 1884, according to the statement made in that year at tariff hearings in Washington, the cost of plate glass to the American consumer approximated only one-half of what it had been before 1879. It was evident that the United States no longer need be helplessly dependent on the glass-making science of Europe."

The basic reason that such an article could be written years later is contained in a letter written by Capt. Ford to his wife in Jeffersonville a few months before actual operations began at Creighton.

The years have made the letter a truly historic document. It follows (the Captain had his own system of spelling and capitalization, and little regard for punctuation.):

Hite Alaghanay Co Pa April 19th 83

My Dear Wife: I Rec'vd your Letter and was Glad to hear that you All Were Well and that you was Pleased With the Grocreys I had Sent. I only Wish I could have Sent More it does me Good to help you All and hope that I may Be Able to Leave A Good home to Each one of My Children So that you Will have A Place that you May Spend the Remaining days of your Life In peace and happiness. I am Ritting this Letter at 5 o'clock Sunday Morning While All are Slepping So that I Can Take it with Me to Pitsburgh and Mail it that you May Recieve it on Monday.

I have to Go and See A Man Who has Promised to be hear a Weak Since and Bring his Boat and Git us Sand as their is No one hear to do the Runing But me and I go No Matter What the Weather is.

I am Still Troubled with My Arm and am not Fealling Well I have Taken Medicen But it does no Good I hope When the Wether Gits Good I will Feel Better.

We have had So much Bad Wether one day Cold then Rain or Snow the Ground is now Covered with Snow. I think the Bad Wether has caused My Troubles With My Arm and My onley Hope for

Relefe is Good Wether. The Ballance here are Well. As to the Works We A-Gitting in Good Shape Making a Splendid Quality of Glass and will Send Samples this Weak. We have the Gass under the Boilers and are now Putting it in the kills (kilns) and have no doubt We will have a nuff to Melt the Glass heat all the Kills and Supply the Boilers and have no use for coal. We have it now In the house in 4 Grates. It is so nice; how Thankful I am for it! Well We have ben Grinding & Smoothing and the Machinery works well. In the Morning we start some of the Pollishers. Have ben Runing them for Several days and they Seem all right and hope they will be when we put Glass on them. Everey thing looks well. All Who have ben here that have taken Stock are highlley Pleased. I sold a Few days since some of our comon Stock for $103 Cash; the Co. have $100,000 of Common Stock to sell for Working Cappital. I had a letter from a Banker in Pitsburgh came last night asking me to bring down Monday $10,000 Stock he would take it and in a Short time would take the Ballance at parr.

Ed Rec'vd a Letter from the Frenchman Last Night Saying he would Start on Monday. We pay him Big Wages but Will have A house Readey for him. Matt Pepper ses Natural Gass Beats them All. We have ten times as maney Calls of Good young men that wants to Learn and Plenty of Girls asking for work. We will have All the houses Full. Have leased 8 of the houses next to the Factory and the owner is to Build 4 more and has comenced them. Mrs Gill Blain & Mother was hear and Spent the day. Her Mother was delited with the Gass. We keep it Going all the Time The Grates are Filled with Pot Shell and I only Wish you Could see it no more Like it was than day is like night We now have Plentey of it.

I should like Emory to leave Jeff (Jeffersonville, Ind.) on Friday Eavening next. I don't often ask him to do Eney thing for me But this he must do . . . I Want him to See the Place. I must now Close Shave and Dress then Breakfast and take the train at 9 and Return at 7

On Last Sunday our Preacher took for his Text by my request made Some Time Since if A man die Shall he Live Again in Job 14th Chapter. He preached a Good Searmon and had a Full house he allways asks about you and I think him a Good Man. Excuse this poor Letter My Love to All

your husband
J. B. Ford

The new plant was christened "The New York Plate Glass Company" in deference to the New York backers, with Albert E. Hughes as president and James R. Shields as secretary.

Early office force at Creighton. Seated, fourth at right, Van Hudepohl; top, third from left, Frank S. Brockett, secretary to Edward Ford.

(For those who might wonder why the founder was not made president, Capt. Ford never would agree to hold an administrative office. He considered himself a builder, and refused to be confined by an office. He preferred to be outside, supervising construction, striding through adjoining fields, strewn with newly arrived machinery and castings, buying up new properties for expansions he planned, mingling with the workers, supervising their work—borrowing a chew of tobacco or a cigar, and often grabbing an amazed employee's shovel or pick to help dig a new foundation—despite his high silk hat, cutaway coat and 70-odd years.)

Within three months after production began at Creighton, the firm name was changed to Pittsburgh Plate Glass Company, unchanged to the present day.

The money loaned to Capt. Ford by New York capitalists, while making it possible to get the new plant under construction, was a drop in the bucket when John Pitcairn, a shrewd moneyed man of Pittsburgh came into the picture.

Already acquainted with the Old Captain, who had sought his counsel about gas, John Pitcairn early became a big stockholder by investing $100,000. Capt. Ford welcomed this new capital, for it enabled him to make his next maneuver as he watched demand for his Creighton plate glass soar, and enlarged the factory.

Without his sons aware of it at the start, the Old Lion began to quietly buy up farm land a half mile away at the edge of Tarentum. Then he organized his own building company, "J. B. Ford & Company."

He built an even larger plant than the one at Creighton. And John Pitcairn, canny Scot that he was, helped with funds to make it possible. (The Captain was using his own personal finances.) Pittsburgh Plate quickly bought the new plant to add to its operations.

Capt. Ford had sold river transportation. Mr. Pitcairn had begun in transportation, too—railroads. Starting with the Pennsylvania at Altoona in his youth, he had

John Pitcairn, largest financial backer of Capt. Ford

Polishing shop, day-shift at Creighton plant. Many of those rouge boys seated in front came on to Rossford to work for Edward Ford, as did many of the older men.
(Photo courtesy Frank Brockett, back row, left, with tie.)

13

The face of the Old Captain near the end of the long, long trail when the three great plants—Creighton, Tarentum and Ford City—all built by Capt. Ford, were profitable operations and the European competition had been greatly reduced, after huge facilities had been made and a higher tariff had been won.

later been a train dispatcher at Fort Wayne, Indiana.

He had been proud of the fact that he was placed in charge of an engine and one car at Harrisburg one morning, on February 22, 1861. He was told to head for Philadelphia. His passenger was President Lincoln.

After serving as superintendent of the Pennsylvania, Mr. Pitcairn began speculating in oil and gas lands, at great profit. In this field, he is said to have become a great admirer of the then skyrocketing John D. Rockefeller.

Boyhood friend of Andrew Carnegie, Pitcairn had opportunity aplenty to acquire a cold-steel shrewdness. He was born in Scotland.

Pitcairn had watched Capt. Ford's operations most carefully, gave freely of advice when Capt. Ford began to make history by pioneering the utilization of gas, the unbelievably cheap fuel of the Valley, at a profit.

No wonder The Old Captain raced along with full steam up. He welcomed Pitcairn's interest in glass. Pitcairn's money had helped to expand operations, and he believed in Mr. Ford's idea for continually increasing production facilities.

Son Edward was president of the company; son Emory was secretary.

In the production end of it, the "New Albany Boys," as Capt. Ford fondly referred to them, were manning the factory in growing numbers. The group included such cronies as John Cooper, his pioneer English grinder; Matt Pepper, his master polisher at New Albany, whom he had now installed as superintendent at Creighton; Marcus D. Wayman, the New Albany mechanic who had already proved to be a genius at making improvements in grinding and polishing equipment; Capt. S. T. Finney, Colonel Harry Sage, John H. Painter and many others.

Capt. Ford was happy in the comfort of his re-grouped family scene, and he was fiercely proud that he had finally solved the formidable problem of quality in production. He was surrounded with easily accessible coal mines, the universal fuel for home and industry

at the time, but he saw in gas the answer to a greatly improved glass.

Capt. Ford was the first man in the world to utilize gas to melt glass!

Not only did this pioneering change cause glass manufacturers on all sides to turn to it, but it encouraged manufacturers in many industries up and down this great industrial valley to switch over to gas.

More glass men came on from New Albany and Jeffersonville and from other communities. Now in his mid 70's, the Old Lion continued to dumbfound people on all sides as he set off a veritable fireworks of crackling industrial enterprises up and down the Valley—a big brick works, a pipe-line company; and as a devastating fire swept through the town's main section four days before Christmas of 1885, Capt. Ford led the movement that gave Tarentum its first pump and hose company.

Incorporated in 1842 with a population of 300, this little town on Bull Creek at the Allegheny, had only 1,200 by 1880. But the Old Captain changed all that. By 1884, Tarentum's population had soared to 4,000, a 300 per cent increase in four years.

Ford City plant erected by Capt. Ford, as it looked years ago from across the Allegheny river . . . stretching a mile along the water front.

It was far past quitting time. Capt. Ford steamed on. He made almost daily trips to Pittsburgh, affectionately known by every engineer, conductor and brakeman on the line; secretly putting young men into business for themselves; providing land for churches to be built; giving to charity right and left; sending money back to New Albany and Jeffersonville to old friends who had helped him when he was down.

But these and other activities were side lines for the Old Lion of the Valley. . . . He went hunting, and 40 miles back up the valley from Pittsburgh, he bagged nine farms near a practically deserted little community variously known as Bonnet and Patterson on the east bank of the river, on the Pittsburgh, Kittaning & Warren Railway.

In rain and snow, he had buggied and walked to search for what he wanted—a site for a town where he could build another big plant. Here in the narrow valley he beat town-site promoters to the one spot wide enough to lay out streets.

And in that year of 1887, the Valley saw new wonders. Capt. Ford built a great new plant and sold it to Pittsburgh Plate. Pitcairn helped provide money, but Capt. Ford was on the ground, hiring men, supervising construction, borrowing a chew of tobacco and a shovel, asking Joe and John and Fred about their babies.

He was having one heluva time for himself, while Edward and Emory shook their heads in their offices back down the Valley.

Congressman John Dalzell, who made the principal address at the statue unveiling ceremonies before 10,000 people.

Ford City, the town was named, in honor of its aged founder. And there it was, in the public park he gave to the community, along with its churches, that 3,000 employees joined in paying homage to their friend and employer.

Special trains moved up the valley to bunting-bedecked Ford City that brisk day of Saturday, November 14, 1891—for the Old Captain's 80th birthday. More than 10,000 people gathered, distinguished business and industrial barons of Pittsburgh, hundreds of workers from towns all along the route of the special trains, and some who had come from New Albany and Jeffersonville for the occasion.

And as the grim old patriarch, with his 85-year-old wife in a chair beside him, and all his family watched the colorful proceedings, Congressman John Dalzell spoke and nine-year-old George Ford pulled the silken cord that unveiled a magnificent bronze likeness of the Father of the American Plate Glass Industry.

It was the idea of the workmen, and 3,000 of them had each volunteered a day's pay to make the statue possible.

What a journey from the tiny log cabin of a Kentucky wilderness to this—the first statue in all American history ever unveiled to a man still living and on hand to hear the roaring, thunderous acclaim.

Capt. Ford couldn't see the dozens of men who suddenly had to blow noses violently as he slowly got up from his chair to respond. His eyes were filled, too.

Bunting-bedecked residence of Mr. Gregg, long time friend of Capt. Ford, dating back to the New Albany days. This view was taken on Saturday, Nov. 14, 1891, during festival surrounding unveiling of statue to Capt. Ford on his 80th birthday.
Left to right, Rev. James A. Ballantyne, who married Hettie Bower Ford, first child of Emory; Mrs. Emory Ford, Mrs. Ballantyne, Miss Gregg, Miss Stella Ford, daughter of Emory and later Mrs. Joseph B. Schlotman, Miss Margaret Ballantyne, Emory L. Ford, Capt. Ford and Mr. Gregg.

Capt. and Mrs. John Baptiste Ford, taken about 1890

CHAPTER 2

Why Edward Ford Came to Toledo

Why would Edward Ford, in the prime of life, give up the presidency of this country's largest and most successful plate glass operation, founded by his father, and start all over again in wholly new surroundings?

It was a matter of policy, really—a determination to stick to a principle, a basic concept of business relations to be maintained between manufacturer and seller, as taught to him by the Father of the American Plate Glass Industry.

After the Ford City works had been placed in operation, the Fords watched the continued buying of additional plate glass plants. They fought it.

Frank S. Brockett, who became Edward Ford's secretary in 1893, commented about the situation some 40 years later.

"That's a long time ago, but I can remember quite well when Edward Ford would return to his office in Creighton after a day of argument in Pittsburgh.

"Mr. Ford would put his feet up on his desk, lean back and light his cigar. I could see he wanted to talk, even though he appeared tired and worn. I was only a young man, inexperienced in glass at the time, but Mr. Ford told me it helped him to talk . . . to sort of blow off steam, I guess.

"It was in President Cleveland's administration, a low-tariff period, and the smaller plate glass plants in the Valley were either closed or operating part time.

"Mr. Pitcairn insisted upon buying those factories, and he proceeded to purchase six of them over a period of time.

"One thing I particularly admired about Edward Ford at this time was his insistence upon sending skilled men into those plants to see what was wrong with the opera-

tions, with orders to improve conditions, despite the fact that he was dead set against their acquisition."

Under Capt. Ford, capitalization had been $2,500,000. After Pitcairn moved in capitalization under reorganization was at a new high—$10,000,000.

Pitcairn's three sons, Raymond, Harold, and Theodore, and two brothers joined the firm. Pitcairn's cousin, Artemus, had long been on the ground to look after the Pitcairn interests. He resided in Tarentum.

Others of the growing group of Pitcairn associates included some former operators of the independent plants that had been purchased.

Frank S. Brocket

Then came a final Difference of Opinion situation. William L. Clause, a young executive from Diamond Plate Glass Company, a Pitcairn acquisition, made a suggestion. "Set up company-owned distributorships," he urged, "take the profits of the local warehouses."

Capt. Ford, when he learned of this plan, bellowed in rage. No company with which he had anything to say would eliminate the independent distributors of his products. This was a time-honored custom, begun when Capt. Ford made glass in New Albany.

But the dour little Scot, friend of Carnegie and admirer of Rockefeller, prevailed. He could easily out-vote the Fords now. And he did.

Many years later, a writer in a national business publication, commented:

"Although Pitcairn readily fell in with Clause's plan, the Fords would have none of it. But Pitcairn, who had been shrewd enough to see a good thing in glass, was also shrewd enough to have held control. The Fords left, organized the Edward Ford Plate Glass Company, which was to merge with others in 1930 to form Libbey-Owens-Ford, Pittsburgh Plate Glass's biggest competitor. Significantly, Pittsburgh still does its own distributing, Libbey-Owens-Ford does not."

Both factions won, but each reached high position in American industry by different roads, the Fords by taking with them as traveling companions the independent glass distributors.

John Pitcairn was 56 when the split occurred in 1897, Capt. Ford was 86.

The Old Captain kept swinging, warrior that he was, and when he severed all connections with Pittsburgh Plate Glass, his shares brought wealth in cash. To Capt. Ford, however, money was not to keep in banks. He was a builder. As the astonishing old gentleman peered toward new horizons, the march of time dealt him a staggering blow.

At midnight, January 12, 1897, Capt. Ford sat grimly beside his wife's bed, holding her withered hand as life ebbed, fluttered and passed, after 91 years.

She had seen so much. She had watched the candle-light flicker across his face as she taught him to read and write. . . . She had watched the sunlight on his face as they unveiled his statue.

Less than two months after Mother Ford's death, Edward resigned as president and general manager, and Emory as secretary.

The embattled Old Captain already had tossed in his heavy holdings of stock.

Having completely severed relations with the business they had founded, where would the Fords go now? The Old Captain had already provided the answer.

When the last cannon had boomed its salute from the hillside at Ford City that eventful day of November 14, 1891, the unveiling of the great bronze statue seemed a fitting and magnificent close to a long business career for the octogenarian.

John B. Ford's wife. (1806-1897)

EARLY FORD CITY OFFICE GROUP

Left to right, seated: P. R. Halbach, chief office clerk; Mark D. Wayman, chief mechanic, who came from New Albany; D. M. Robinson, general manager; John Ferguson, standing.

Left to right, standing: Ferd Reisgen, clerk; Al Ferguson, office boy; Art Gillespie, office boy; J. C. Woodward, clerk; S. J. Robinson, general manager of clerks; Joseph Henry, timekeeper, later paymaster at Rossford; C. F. McGarvey, clerk; Edward C. Bowers, master mechanic, clerk and receiving clerk (father of the late Eddie Bowers and plant manager at Rossford, 1915-1934; W. J. Carson, first assistant clerk; W. J. Boggs, clerk.

Everybody took it for granted, except the octogenarian.

For fully a year before they had erected the monument intended to mark the end of the trail in a blaze of glory for him, the Old Lion had been on the prowl again.

He had been making secret trips while his sons wondered and worried. Where was he going, what was he doing? "He's going to lose his shirt again, just like he did back in New Albany," some of the folk grumbled with affectionate anxiety.

The Old Captain kept his own counsel, grinning a bit as the months rolled on, occasionally slipping aboard a train at Pittsburgh, off at Toledo and aboard again for Detroit. There he took the "local" for Wyandotte, sleepy hamlet on the Detroit river. If the "local" had left, he took a buggy—rain or snow.

Why? Why was he prowling around this farmland south of the town? And why did he buy a farm because it had a salt water well—abandoned in disgust by drillers who had sought gas?

He was after soda ash. It long had rankled him, back to his New Albany days, that he had to buy one of his most important ingredients for glass—soda ash—from foreign interests. At Creighton, Tarentum and Ford City, soda ash still had to be purchased from sources owned by Europeans. Besides, he hated to buy anything in quantity that he felt could be produced by himself and his associates.

Once he had purchased the acreage at Wyandotte, after making sure that abundant layers of salt beds were underground, Capt. Ford placed his grandson and namesake, John B., (Edward's son) in charge. Under his grandfather's guidance, the young man made several trips to England to get chemists.

After the new organization, Michigan Chemical, (later changed to Michigan Alkali Company) was a going concern, Capt. Ford capitalized it at $1,000,000. In 1896, he lifted it to $2,500,000.

Edward Ford headed the company, with his son as vice president and general manager, and Edward's son-in-law, Dr. G. P. MacNichol, as treasurer.

Left to right, John B., and his infant son, John B. III; Edward Ford and Capt. Ford

Following the break with Pittsburgh Plate Glass one year later, The Fords left the Allegheny forever—all except the Old Captain. He preferred to remain in the Valley of his greatest conquest, among his old cronies and the glass workers who looked upon him with great affection. Yes, here he would stay, in the fine old mansion on the bank of the river, making occasional trips to Wyandotte to advise and counsel.

This new business at Wyandotte, already turning out endless tons of soda ash—most of it now being purchased by Pittsburgh Plate Glass—and bearing promise of innumerable allied by-products for supplying to a wide variety of American industries, something the Old Lion had foreseen early in his prowlings in the area.

This business he intended as a legacy to his family, with no outside interferences that might lead to an explosion such as had so recently occurred on the banks of the Allegheny.

Edward Ford was president of Michigan Chemical, but he was not a chemical man. Plate glass was his love. It was in his blood, had been since his youth.

On one of the Old Captain's trips to Wyandotte, Edward sought his father's advice. The old gentleman listened attentively. His face didn't show it, but inside he glowed. In his characteristically gruff voice, he answered:

"Well, Edward, you are a wealthy man now. Start your own plate glass company."

The Old Lion got up from his chair, brushed vigorously at imaginary dust on the seat of his trousers, eyed his stalwart son and added: "Well, I gotta git goin'—why don't you?"

CHAPTER **3**

Edward Ford — The Founder

Edward Ford was born January 21, 1843, in the back-woods settlement of Greenville, Indiana.

Chicago was 10 years old, Bunker Hill monument had just been dedicated. Fremont's expedition sighted Pike's Peak and the second wagon train had just headed into the west from Independence, Missouri. It would be another year before Sam Morse was ready to send the first message by wire—from Washington to Baltimore.

New York City felt pretty good. It had just started its first water system, bringing water from Croton piped through hollow logs. Another 10 years would find Peter Cooper forging the first iron beams for American buildings.

When he was 11, Edward's parents moved into New Albany, where he was educated in the public schools. After graduating from Bryant & Stratton Commercial College in Indianapolis, he returned to New Albany. He clerked for a time in a small book store, but soon filtered into his father's various water-front enterprises.

From bookkeeping in his father's steamboat office, Edward was put in charge of the steamer, Atlantic, a Twin Stack stern-wheeler plying between Louisville and New Orleans. Frequent passengers were Evelyn Carter Penn and her mother. Edward Ford married the pretty Kentucky girl from Louisville in 1864, when she was 19 and he was 20.

The young wife died seven years later, leaving Edward with a six-year-old daughter, Mary; and four-year-old John B. Ford, named for his grandfather.

This was only a year after Capt. Ford had succeeded in making plate glass in the small experimental plant. When the glass operations continued to prove unprofitable, Edward took a position with the Columbus (Ohio) Window Glass Company. It was about this time that he met 19-year-old Caroline Ross of Zanesville, Ohio. They were married in 1872.

Mrs. Caroline Ross Ford

21

THOSE WERE THE DAYS

Hite's Station (Creighton) to join his father after Capt. Ford had acquired property and was ready to start building. Edward was put in charge of construction. Edward's last child, George Ross Ford, was born at Creighton in 1882, just before the new plant got under way.

"Alike as two peas." "A chip off the old block." Those and other old bromides fit Capt. Ford and his son, Edward. Both were stocky, heavy-set, fast on their feet; and both were highly production-minded. Edward's brother, Emory, was the sales-minded member of the family.

In his long tenure as first president and general manager of Pittsburgh Plate Glass Company, Edward Ford was always a familiar figure "out in the Works," first to be on hand when a break-down occurred, often lending a hand to repair equipment, and constantly seeking ways to improve mechanical operations.

The gem-like gleam of his finished product, the shouting of the men as huge plates of glass were lifted and swung from the polishing tables, the din of machinery— all this was symphonic music to his ears. No wonder he felt strange and alone in the land of quiet chemistry at Wyandotte.

Their first child, Laura, (Mrs. G. P. MacNichol, Sr.) was born in Columbus in 1874. Mr. Ford rejoined his father and brother, Emory, at Jeffersonville when the Captain resigned from Louisville Plate Glass Company to try again with his own plant.

Edna Ford (the late Mrs. W. W. Knight, Sr.) was born in Jeffersonville in 1879. Edward moved his family to

Edward Ford's residence at Creighton, facing the Allegheny river. (Capt. Ford's home was nearby.) At left, holding tennis racquet, is Edna Ford, later Mrs. W. W. Knight; seated nearby, Laura Ford; George Ross Ford, seated on bicycle, right.

CHAPTER 4

Rossford is Born

When Edward Ford arrived in Toledo he found a city of 150,000 that had mushroomed from 13,000 in less than 30 years. There were 24 railroads. Three passenger steamers left Toledo daily.

Week-end mecca was Hotel Victory at Put-in-Bay, awesome in its sprawling magnificence, largest west of New York. While a band puffed and perspired in spangled hot uniforms, bumptious swains strolled the beach in handlebar mustaches and navy blue bathing suits that flapped far below their knees.

Imposing homes were being built for $750. Folk were still awed by the Apperson brothers' one-cylinder automobile that had just succeeded in attaining six miles an hour; and the United States Army announced the purchase of three automobiles for use of its officers, explaining that mules could be hitched on if the cars refused to run. McKinley was president.

The Alaskan gold rush was on, plans were being made for Admiral Dewey's victory reception in Washington and rumor had it that rural free mail service was spreading in Ohio.

Golden Rule Sam Jones was mayor of Toledo. The Boody House (where the Owens-Illinois Building now stands) was the mecca for distinguished guests from faraway places. A block away, in Conley & Patterson's restaurant, diners complained of high prices. Six Blue Point oysters cost 15 cents. A plate of beef was a dime; an eight-course luncheon, 60 cents.

Mr. Ford's first business contact in Toledo was with Rathbun Fuller of the law firm of Swayne, Hayes, Fuller & Tyler. They became close friends and long-time business associates.

Attorney Fuller introduced Glassmaker Ford to Irving B. Hiett, who, according to his modest advertisement,

Breaking ground for Edward Ford's new plant at Rossford

dealt in "Real Estate, loans, fire insurance, investments, business and dwelling property, building lots, fine residences and neat cottages."

The threesome carriaged up and down the river. Finally, on the east bank, Edward Ford found what he liked, and negotiations were started. Mr. Ford originally purchased 173 acres.

Surveyors began squinting through their instruments, but Mr. Ford insisted upon waiting until the farmers had harvested their crops. On the last day of August, 1898, the first spade of soil was turned for the new plant.

Yellow construction shanties of A. Bentley & Sons began to polka dot the landscape, horse-drawn scoops bit deep into the land and dozens of teams of horses and mules leaned into their collars as they strained with great rumbling wagon loads of lumber and brick, steel and stone.

Carpenters and brick masons, machinists and day laborers swarmed in, and in the fields where grain and fruit orchards had reigned, there arose factory walls, and monstrous machinery slowly came to life.

Coming of the Glass Works created great excitement in the rural communities. Farmers brought their families in big wagons to picnic and stare at the strange buildings. Smart carriages, and long lines of buggies filled the narrow country road leading from Toledo and Perrysburg as families came to peek and wander through the fenceless grounds on Sunday afternoons.

The summer of 1899 found the Works about ready to make glass. One furnace was placed in operation at the start.

First cast of plate glass was made on October 28, 1899, but the first shipment was delayed purposely by Edward Ford.

It was made on November 17—in the presence of a distinguished visitor—Capt. Ford.

A load of plate glass was prepared with great care. Capt. Ford, Edward and a group of associates stood around just outside the office. President Ford walked back and forth, chewing his familiar black El Verso, glancing back at the warehouse nervously, then at his aged father, imperturbable as usual, joking with old cronies.... A man stood near, ready with a chair, in case those old legs should falter.

A span of mules hitched to a large wagon clopped into view. A dozen men eyed the team, the proud driver, Ed Walters, and the big racks of glass. The driver kept right on, eyes glued upon his mules. They turned left out on the road, headed for Toledo.

Capt. Ford and President Ford stood rigid, watching until the team and wagon were swallowed by a ravine.

Oldtimers, stealing a glance at the pair, faded away. The sight of the moist eyes of those two silent men, father and son, tightened their throats.

"Gawdamighty," growled one of the men with deep reverence, "what a wonderful way to honor the Old Captain's eighty-eighth birthday."

This bird's-eye of Edward Ford Plate Glass Company's [orig]inal plant, as it appeared in 1900, was created from t[wo] sources of information; an early engineering drawin[g]

As the Twentieth Century neared, the world and the nation stood on the cliffs of high promise. So did Rossford.

Many a west-bound Pennsylvania locomotive hauled freight cars crammed with furniture, cows and family pets as plate glass men came on from Creighton, Tarentum and Ford City.

Many had never known anything but the hills of Pennsylvania. And as they came streaking across the flat lands of Ohio, the women and their children were wide-eyed and eager—heading west to rejoin the Fords. It would be good to be back in the folds of Fordiana.

No man in America could have been busier than Edward Ford in those formative days. With his own money he had bought the land, purchased the materials,

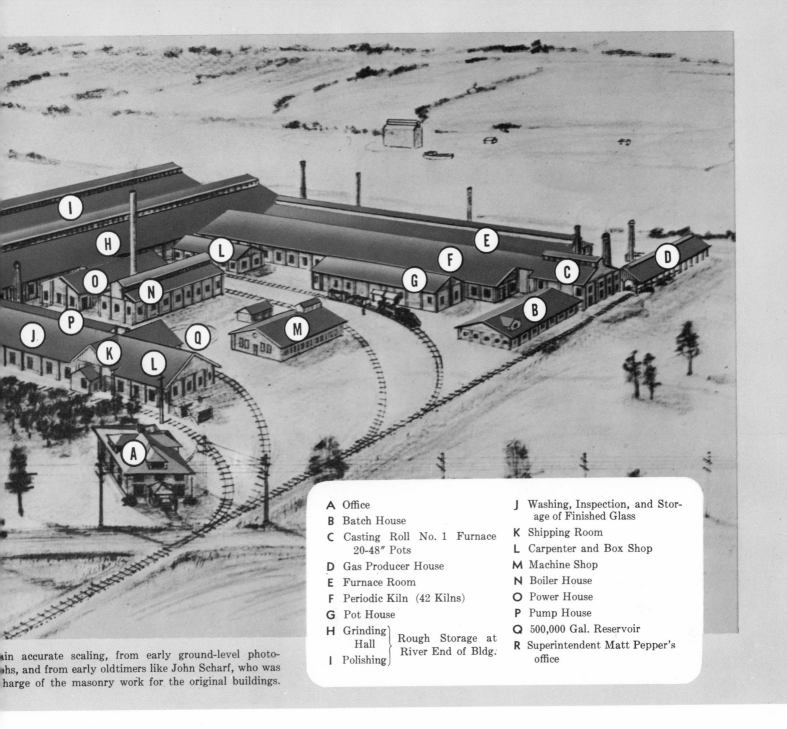

...ain accurate scaling, from early ground-level photo-
...ohs, and from early oldtimers like John Scharf, who was
...harge of the masonry work for the original buildings.

A	Office	J	Washing, Inspection, and Storage of Finished Glass
B	Batch House	K	Shipping Room
C	Casting Roll No. 1 Furnace 20-48″ Pots	L	Carpenter and Box Shop
D	Gas Producer House	M	Machine Shop
E	Furnace Room	N	Boiler House
F	Periodic Kiln (42 Kilns)	O	Power House
G	Pot House	P	Pump House
H	Grinding Hall } Rough Storage at River End of Bldg.	Q	500,000 Gal. Reservoir
I	Polishing	R	Superintendent Matt Pepper's office

paid the wages and all the construction costs—all before
he formed a company. He had financed a railroad spur,
from the old Cincinnati, Hamilton and Dayton mainline
tracks into his property. This line, christened the Rossford & Toledo Railroad Company, formed the north
boundary of the Glass Works at that time. Mr. Ford
incorporated the line on October 11, 1898, with the
following, in addition to himself: Rathbun Fuller, William
P. Tyler, Matt Pepper, Thomas A. Taylor and Frank H.
Tanner. Capitalization was $10,000, at $100 per share.

Not until after the first successful cast had been made
late in October of 1899, did Ford incorporate the glass
works, waiting until he was sure that everything was
working properly.

On November 11, 1899, the Edward Ford Plate Glass
Company was formed, with these incorporators, in addition to Mr. Ford:

Morrison W. Young, then president of the Blade
Printing & Paper Co., 316 Gardner Bldg.; Fred J.
Reynolds, of Reynolds Brothers, Grain Commissioners,
Produce Exchange Bldg.; Edwin Jackson, then president
of the Merchants National Bank (of which pioneer Noah
H. Swayne was vice president); and Attorney Rathbun
Fuller.

The company was launched with a capitalization of
$2,000,000 divided into 20,000 shares of $100 each. The
incorporators, acting as the first board of directors, with
Leonard S. Johnson, auditor of the Toledo Stone Glass
Sand Co., added to the directorate, met in Mr. Fuller's

office, 624 Spitzer Bldg., on November 23, and elected the following first officers of the new company:

Edward Ford, president and treasurer.

John B. Ford, (Edward's son and head of Ford-formed Michigan Chemical Co., Wyandotte) vice president.

Andrew Brymer, secretary.

As an individual, Mr. Ford now turned over all his holdings to the new company, the board of directors voting to purchase for cash and stock.

On January 14, 1901, after one full year of production, the personnel of the original glass company directorate changed. Replacing Morrison Young, Fred Reynolds and Edwin Jackson were Dr. George P. MacNichol, (Edward's son-in-law) and Matt Pepper.

This group was re-elected in 1902, but Mr. MacNichol replaced Andrew Brymer (who had served part of 1898 and all of 1899) as secretary. Mr. MacNichol also was elected treasurer.

At the ground-breaking ceremonies, on August 31, 1899, Edward Ford handed a shovel to a spick-and-span little gentleman whose sparkling black Alpaca suit, well-polished shoes and black derby stood out in those surroundings like a lone black raspberry in a bowl of milk.

As Mr. Ford handed the shovel to the meticulously dressed man chosen for this honor, their eyes met for an instant in deep understanding and appreciation of this moment.

"Push that spade down deep, Matt," Edward smiled at him.

Matthias R. Pepper was one of a small group of men who had helped Capt. John B. Ford produce his first plate glass successfully at New Albany in 1869.

Born in Birmingham, England, Matt had arrived in New Albany when he was 24 with his young wife and two children—Sarah Jane, who married a Ford pioneer glass worker, Charles Kier, in Creighton in 1886; and John, a booker in the Edward Ford plant and who died

at Rossford in 1915. (Mrs. Kier was still living at the age of 89 in New Kensington, Pa., in 1956.)

Matt, Jr., born in New Albany in 1873, was associated with the Fords for many years as a glass cutter and beveler. He died in 1936. Priscilla, born in New Albany in 1875, married Otis Warner, another Ford employee, at Rossford in 1905. She died in 1942.

Lillian Alberta, fifth and final child of Matt Pepper, was born in Creighton in 1885, soon after Capt. Ford opened his plant there. She married Benjamin Brown at Rossford in 1914.

Mrs. Lillian Pepper Brown, daughter of Matt

After Capt. Ford's epochal comeback at Creighton, he sent Matt Pepper to England and Belgium several times to recruit skilled workers. In charge of early operations at Creighton as foreman of the all-important polishing department, Mr. Pepper became manager of the Ford City Works when it was completed.

He stayed there until Edward Ford invited him to rejoin him at Rossford.

When he resigned at Pittsburgh Plate to join Edward Ford, Mr. Pepper was presented with a gold watch engraved as follows: "Presented to Matthias R. Pepper in appreciation of his faithful service and contributions to the Plate Glass Industry."

Matt, who had polished the first light of plate glass ever made in America, after his father-in-law, John Cooper, had ground it for Capt. Ford, was credited with several inventions within the industry.

When he died, November 8, 1928, in the home of his daughter, Mrs. Otis A. Warner, Sr., Eagle Point Road, he had completed 67 years in plate glass, having started with Pilkington Brothers in England when he was 15. Fifty-eight of those years were in almost continuous service with the Fords.

He lies in Manor cemetery in Ford City, where he was a member of the Methodist Church, one of several churches built upon property donated by Capt. Ford.

Matt Pepper, Capt. Ford's first polisher (at New Albany) and first plant manager at Rossford

CHAPTER 5

First Families and First Glass

Months before the first cast of plate in the new plant, Edward Ford began building houses for the influx of glass men and their families.

A dry spring enabled construction of the first group of dwellings to start on April 11, 1899. Edward, having watched how his father had pushed the construction of houses and schools and churches on the farmlands surrounding his plant at Creighton, and later in the fields surrounding the Ford City plant, now followed the same procedure.

He led a movement for a Board of Education. Its first meeting was held May 31, 1899. He made possible the first school and in it were held the first preaching and religious services—less than three months after the boilers were fired up in the new plant.

There is a bushel basketful of Firsts surrounding those embryo years. Many of the men and women who came to Rossford first have passed on, but hundreds of their descendants are there now.

From Creighton, among the first were the Matthew Bertrands, J. H. Cauffields, Jacob Heinrichs, Charles Kier, Jules LaHote, August Leidigk and sons.

From Tarentum: Gustave Berkiss, John Bialett, Charles Kapp, William Kummer (who managed the first hotel at Rossford), Joseph Mainz, Sam Mannell, Peter Schings, the Strickers, Peter Rossler, Aaron Robbins, Jeff Venable, Bert Henderson.

From Ford City: William Burns, Edward Callahan, the Campbell family, John Connors, Mrs. John Cooper (her husband was with Capt. Ford at New Albany at the very start); Vincent Fildes, Richard Hazlett, Robert Hunter, the Edward, Henry and William King families; Frank Krakau, Sr., John Kimmell, August LaHote, Harvey Linweber, Matt Pepper, Sr. and Jr.; Thomas Pierpoint, Joseph Smith, Sam Westfall, and Louis Zerney.

Among the first families to arrive also were those of John and George Sullivan of Bowling Green, and Adolph Heidrich of Rocky Ridge.

Many of those just listed were the "first foremen." Here they are, as of 1899:

Pot House............Frank Krakau
Mixing department....John Sullivan, George Sullivan
Rouge department.....John Bialett
Emery department.....John Connors
Casting hall..........Thomas J. (Jeff) Venable
Grinding department...Edward King, Harvey Linweber
Polishing department..Vincent Fildes
Laying department....Richard Hazlett
Wareroom............Matthew Bertrand

EARLY OFFICE GROUP

Left to right: Claude Lewis, John Kuntz, Mary Thraves, Van Hudepohl, Dr. MacNichol, Edward Ford; back of Edward Ford's left shoulder, George Ross Ford. See if you can identify any of the others

FOUR KINGS

Left to right: Ed, Walter, William H. King and John. Photo taken by Walter in his home about 1904. He snapped the picture by using a string attached to his finger.

Brick-laying.........Gus Berkiss
Carpenter shop.......Sam Mannell
Master mechanic......John Kountz
Electrical engineers....William Perkins
Time keeper.........Joseph Henry
Purchasing..........J. H. Cauffield
Drafting............Curtice Long
Office..............Sylvanus S. Hudepohl

Edward Ford's plant turned out 23,705 square feet of finished polished plate glass in November (a partial month of production, of course) and in December production rose to 48,121 square feet—with only one furnace in operation.

There was much to be thankful for that Christmas of 1899. Old friends and many families had been reunited from the Valley of the Allegheny to the Valley of the Maumee, and as a new century approached, a familiar scene was on view—Christmas trees in the little plant, singing of carols as mothers and daughters were invited into the factory—to see and to sing, and to take home Christmas gifts.

Many an aged retired man resting comfortably in his own home today in Rossford, and many of their grown sons thank Edward Ford for personally urging his employees to invest their savings in homes.

Those who had to wait to buy, rented Ford-built cottages at low charges, with water and electric lights from the plant furnished free. Any employee, for $100 down, could buy a lot or house on a long-time payment plan.

Every man who bought property owned by Edward Ford signed a deed that included a clause prohibiting forever the sale of intoxicating liquor upon the premises.

Rare view—Edward Ford, with his two sons

CHAPTER 6

"This Land Is Best."

Before moving further with Edward Ford into his first full year of production, let's look back to those days when the land was a trackless forest, where Indians and wolves both stalked their prey on the very ground where you now see well-kept lawns and gardens.

Early settlers came in slowly, armed only with dreams and courage and determination. Many of them left indelible marks upon the Rossford of today.

There was Gabriel Crane, for example. Born on a farm near Albany, New York, in 1800, he couldn't forget the gossip of strangers he overheard in a village inn near his home. One of them, returning East, had said: "Out West, beyond the mountains, lies the most wonderful soil I have ever seen. It is beside a river they call the Maumee."

At 20, Gabriel Crane could wait no longer. He walked all the way, coming in over the forbidding Black Swamp Road (now Route 20) to the little settlement of Perrysburg. He explored the entire area northward to Maumee Bay. He fingered the soil, tasted it, an Old World custom of his father's. Yes, this land was best.

Gabe began to buy land from the government. After a time his domain spread southward from Oregon Road to the present Libbey-Owens-Ford Thermopane plant, with frontage on the river and eastward beyond Wales Road.

Gabriel Crane

He came to know Peter Navarre, the famous scout, only 15 years his elder. He cut down the great trees, slowly clearing tiny patches for farming. In his fifties, Gabe helped to lay brick for Toledo's Oliver House—more than a century ago.

He built the first frame house in the area, now the site of the Thermopane plant. He raised four children—James, Henry, Amos and Clara.

Who could guess that one day the lives of his children and grandchildren would become entwined with those of a lad just then running away from home in far-off Kentucky!

Clara, born in 1841, lived to sell some of the Crane land to Edward Ford. She could well remember the wolves, and how her father, Gabriel, on occasion risked his life to get a pelt for which he would receive as high as $1.25.

Clara's mother, living as a bride in a cabin on the site of the Thermopane plant, often was startled as she sat darning or sewing after sundown—Indians staring through the tiny window at her—demanding food. She could recall a tribe of Indians camping in the ravine where trucks of Edward Ford Plate used to get stuck regularly years later, the ravine that marked the end of the old Oak street car line on Miami street, and which, now filled by Libbey-Owens-Ford, marks the north boundary of Rossford.

House built by George Davis, father of the Rossford veteran, Warren Davis. The house was erected in 1856—42 years before a small community began to grow beside the new Glass Works, built when Edward Ford was a child of 13 in Greenville, Indiana. When streets were laid out in Rossford, this house became 156 Bacon Street.

Gabe's eldest son, James, had four children—Isaac, Harvey, Irving and Mary Ann, mother of Mrs. Clyde (Mary Ann) Rowley, 318 Forest Drive, Eagle Point.

Isaac and Irving had a big dairy farm on Wales Road. A daughter of Isaac resides in the old James Crane brick homestead, second house north of the Thermopane plant on Miami street. The L-O-F Oldtimers annual picnic is held in the James Crane woods.

Gabe's second son, Henry, had five children—Frank, Daniel, Harry, Louise, and Grace. Louise is Mrs. E. E. Teegardin, 1829 Miami street. Grace married a son of the founder of the Wachter Shoe Company of Toledo. Her husband was born on the present site of Lasalle's store. Both reside at 561 Oak street, Dundee, Michigan.

Gabe's third son, Amos, also had five children, including Eunice and Carl.

Eunice married William Barthold, 416 Oregon Road.

Carl Crane, grandson of Gabriel, is Rossford manager of the International Mineral & Chemical Company, located between the Thermopane plant and the Larro Milling Company.

Carl well remembers the coming of the Ford Glass Works. His most exciting boyhood recollection was the day a tire blew out on Edward Ford's big brown Peerless in front of the plant. He answered the chauffeur's request for assistance with eagerness.

Dusty from head to foot from his wrestling with the stubborn clincher rim, young Carl backed away, exhausted but triumphant, and throbbing with his thrilling introduction to the mechanical age. He heard a deep voice: "Son, come here . . . hold out your hand."

Crane nearly fainted when he saw the bright coins in his grubby little paw. He had never seen so much money. Edward Ford had given him 75 cents!

Years later, in the early 1920's, he had another Ford experience he recalls with a smile. He won the contract to build the long driveway that winds through the trees from East River Road to the river-bank home of one of

Edward Ford's grandsons, George P. MacNichol, Jr., now president of Libbey-Owens-Ford.

Carl recalls a day when the land just back of the Thermopane plant was ploughed in 1914. Carl found many arrow heads, stone knives, bullets and a miscellany of the long ago.

The widow of Isaac Crane, dairy-operator grandson of Gabriel, recalled Edward Ford passing her place often in his horse 'n' buggy.

"He always waved," she said.

Gabriel Crane died at the age of 82, sixteen years before the arrival of the Glass Works at Rossford. He rests in Willow Cemetery.

A mile or so south of the Cranes, along Grassy Creek where Eagle Point Road turns toward the Maumee, lived another pre-Rossford pioneer, Doria (pronounced Doe-rye-ah) Tracy.

A lumberman, Doria came from Massachusetts in 1867, in the post Civil War westward migration. He bought land near the mouth of Grassy Creek, intending to build wharves and float logs downriver. When he discovered this was impractical, he bought land further down and built wharves at the spot which later became the B & O docks, land which in recent years was purchased by Libbey-Owens-Ford.

One of Doria's children, Katharine, born in Caneadea, New York in 1855, and only 10 years old when her parents arrived in this area, married Julius G. Lamson, co-founder of The Lamson Brothers Company.

Julius, a young clerk boarding at 101 Summit street at the time, used to row across the Maumee to court Katharine Tracy. After they were married in 1878, the

Pioneer Doria Tracy, 1808-1894

William N. Tracy

William Tracy home. Now site of Catholic church in Rossford

Lamsons lived for a time on Miami street, a block north of Brown road.

Katharine Tracy Lamson was the mother of three daughters—Elizabeth, who married the late Rev. Harrie R. Chamberlain; Miriam, who married the late Sidney D. Vinnedge, and Katharine, who married Charles E. Swartzbaugh, Jr., Toledo manufacturer. She died in 1950.

Katharine's brother, Frank Edwin Tracy, who became associated with his father, Doria, in lumbering in the Rossford area, raised six children. One of them, Katharine, niece of Katharine Tracy Lamson, married Edwin C. Law, in 1909. He was a divisional freight agent for the B & O at the time. Katharine Tracy Law is the mother of Edwin T. Law, manager of window glass sales for Libbey-Owens-Ford.

William N. Tracy, another son of Doria, who took over the original 57 acres purchased by his father, became a widely known fruit grower and left many descendants as a result of his two marriages.

His first three children, by Sarah Foster, were Clarence, Ernest, and Doria.

Clarence married Anna Messer, had three children. One of them, Jeannette Ann, married Ralph M. Barnes, of the general offices of Libbey-Owens-Ford's East Broadway plant.

William's second wife, Estella I. Bowers, is related to Dr. Merlin Bowers of Perrysburg. There were two children, Robert and Ruth. Robert, a graduate of Massachusetts Institute of Technology, married Olive Burnham of Nova Scotia, in 1922, while at M. I. T. There were two sons by this marriage—Robert Burnham

Tracy, a Yale graduate, now a member of L-O-F's Thermopane plant; and Doria Richard. Robert Tracy Sr., died in 1938. His widow married Ralph Farnsworth, head of L-O-F's order department, in 1945.

Near the Tracy farm, across East River Road, between Grassy Creek and northward to Glenwood Road, was the farm of Elliott M. Warner, long a distinguished resident of Rossford, friend of both Captain and Edward Ford.

Born in 1844, at Congress, Ohio, near Oberlin, son of an itinerant minister, Mr. Warner came to the Rossford area in 1875. (He had served in Company B, 144th OVI, Civil War.)

Warner became widely known as a fruit grower. On land now occupied by Rossford High School, its field house and ball park, Mr. Warner had annual yields averaging 500 bushels of peaches, 400 of pears, 125 of plums, 100 of apples, 60 of cherries, large quantities of currants, quinces and gooseberries, and an average of four tons of grapes.

Many a Rossford oldster of today was taught his or her Sunday School lesson by Warner in the little red school house that used to stand at the junction of Eagle Point and River Roads. The children usually met once a week at the Warner residence and the following week at the William Tracys for Sunday School hymn practice.

This branch of the Tracy family had much in common with Warner. Both highly successful fruit growers, they served long terms as Ross Township trustees; both served as presidents of the old Lucas County Horticultural Society, an influential organization of the day, and their wives held high offices in the Floricultural Society.

Mr. Warner, who attended Oberlin College, and his wife, who attended Painesville College on Lake Erie, were widely influential in the social and religious life of the Rossford area for many years.

They had three children—Howard, 1872-1954, known for his Rossford grocery for many years; Otis, who married Priscilla Pepper, daughter of Matt; and Jennie. Otis worked in the Rossford grinding department for a short time. He died in 1950.

Jennie, born in 1876, in what became Rossford, married the late Harvey M. Linweber in 1901, after Linweber came on with many others from Ford City, where he had been night superintendent of the grinding department.

Linweber worked for the Fords for about 15 years, later joining the Toledo Shipbuilding Company for a few years, then retiring to the Warner homestead on the north bank of Grassy Creek, where only three acres were left of the original Warner property, after Elliott sold more and more land to the expanding community.

Elliott Warner died in 1930, three weeks short of his 87th milestone.

Elliott Warner

George Hubbell house, on land now occupied by the Twin-Grind plant. It was between the river and the end of the old Oak Street carline. Inset shows original house, on same property, later became a storage shed.

CHAPTER 7

The Twentieth Century Rolls In

Gunfire and kisses, rowdyism and prayers, shouting sleigh riders and solemn church bells ushered in 1900.

What was ahead? Old men voiced dire predictions. Young folk flirted, married, and raised families. Expanding educational facilities turned out record-breaking throngs of bright-eyed graduates.

The Spanish-American War had ended. President McKinley was walking straight toward his assassination, and the reckless hero of San Juan Hill, Rough-Rider Teddy Roosevelt, was riding toward the White House.

A Stanley Steamer climbed Mount Washington and Alexander Winton drove his newly invented automobile from Cleveland to New York in four days to exhibit in New York City's first automobile show, held in Madison Square Garden.

In Rossford, Edward Ford was seated at his desk, black El Verso clamped between his jaws, his mind leafing the mental pages of the chapters to be written from here on.

On the first day of the new century's first decade, Edward Ford was well aware that he faced gargantuan problems.

He had one lone plate glass furnace in operation. He had several competitors, but none equalled the leader. Pittsburgh Plate Glass Company; his father had founded it, he himself had managed it for 15 years.

One furnace against so many! Mr. Ford stared at the walls of his new office as he weighed the possibilities.

No farmer ever attempted to count each straw in his stack, and no one ever kept count of each progressive step made at the Edward Ford Plate Glass Works, but there were interesting symbols of advancements in the early stages of that first decade.

Mr. Ford changed from driving his own horse 'n' buggy to a coachman and surrey, then to chauffeur and automobile. His first span of mules for deliveries to Toledo jobbers gave way to chain-driven trucks.

Edward was nearing 60; his eldest son, John B. Ford, was in his late thirties, guiding his grandfather-created Michigan Alkali to new achievements at Wyandotte, and serving as one of the directors of the Rossford glass works; Edward's youngest son, George, was 18.

Mr. Ford eyed his son with both affection and concern as George approached young manhood. When he was

The Chocolate Drop. That's what the family dubbed Edward Ford's magnificent dark brown Peerless. The chauffer is Otto Johnson.

One of George Ross Ford Sr's. racy hot-rod jobs. Right hand drive, too.

George's age, Edward had charge of a union riverboat troop carrier, engaged in the dangerous business of sliding past Confederate shore batteries.

George wasn't too much interested in glass. His hobby was motorcycles and automobiles. There was an amusing side to this situation. In his persistent efforts to get his father to buy him an automobile, George pleaded that streetcar riding made him "seasick." In an effort to prove his contention, George often got off the swaying Oak street car and by supreme efforts in holding his breath until he was red-faced, he could manage to retch and strangle. To his deep chagrin, this performance always left his father completely unimpressed.

But young George had a typical Ford trait—tenacity. He got an automobile before his father owned one.

The first half of that first decade was just over, however, when young George found himself in a bear-trap. According to his own wails to some of his pals in the factory, it was a conspiracy led by his father, his elder half brother, John B. of Wyandotte and a few others.

George was elected to the board of directors! That was on August 1, 1905, when George was only 23.

While he was still trying to figure out ways to untangle himself from this new responsibility, George found the rope tightening further. When Claude L. Lewis, a production man in the plant, was elected a director to replace the ailing Matt Pepper, now nearing 60, George was elected treasurer of the company, with Lewis as secretary.

Other changes were taking place, too. From 100 homes and 600 employees in 1903, there were many new houses, additional streets, more employees. And Edward Ford had managed to get a post office for Rossford. (The first money order sold in Rossford was on January 6, 1903.)

Grief diluted success for a time. Capt. Ford died at his residence in Creighton on May 1, 1903, aged 92. Thousands of workers and their wives in New Albany, Jeffersonville, Creighton, Tarentum, Ford City and Rossford mourned. Memorial services were held in a dozen communities and newspapers printed editorials about the Old Lion of American industry.

Excerpt from one: ". . . he will leave lasting monuments behind him, great industries that give employment to thousands of men. He has done much for labor, for it was through labor that he came to his wealth and influence. Indeed Capt. Ford has written an important chapter in the history of American industry, and the marvel of it as an achievement and the conviction of it as an eloquent lesson is the fact that he did it when he had almost passed the normal span of life. He was in the common acceptance an old man when he started upon the work that marks an epoch in American industry, that has built towns, formed communities, and given vast impetus to labor and vital economic products."

Detroit Journal: "No greater endorsement of American pluck, perseverance and will power can be found than this, nor a greater monument of a life well spent."

CAPT. JOHN B. FORD
1811-1903

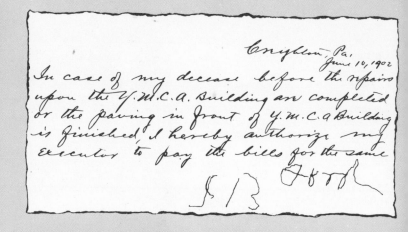

One of Capt. Ford's last signatures

Improvements in grinding and polishing methods were being made by Edward Ford at Rossford from time to time, and new buildings to handle expanding production. Ford saw the need for someone to take charge of the traffic problem.

Typical of the expansion of the times, Edward Ford went beyond the world of glass for a man. He found him, and in a logical place —at a desk in the freight office of the old Lake Shore & Michigan Southern Railroad, across the river at the Middle Grounds. The man was Clark E. Husted.

Mr. Husted had come to Toledo in 1890 from Buffalo with his father, Giles E. Husted, freight agent

Clark E. Husted, about 1907-8

for the New York Central Railroad. After high school, Clark got into railroading. His first job was calling crews at Airline Junction, often riding his bicycle at midnight to awaken conductors and brakemen for special runs. He had advanced to the freight office rate desk when the call from Edward Ford came.

Mr. Husted was 26 when he became traffic manager for Edward Ford Plate in 1906.

One of the first office girls to be employed by the Ford Works was Mary Thraves. Beginning in 1902, she started what ended up as 43 years of continuous service.

She came to know Edward Ford very well, serving as secretary and taking charge of the growing order department.

Before the decade had ended, Mary Thraves was called upon to act temporarily in the capacity of sales manager to handle details at the plant, an assignment she did well, and at double pay during a three-month emergency occasioned by the death of George W. DeMaid, second sales manager of the company.

As business expanded, with new office help added from time to time, many questions had to be answered, and the phrase, "Ask Mary," became a by-word and a tradition.

From its inception, the Edward Ford Plate Glass Company was a one-family organization at the control level, and Edward Ford intended to keep it that way. Only in this manner could he insist upon selling his products in the way he and his father had insisted upon— through independent glass distributor companies. This method had prevailed until the difference of opinion occurred in Pittsburgh Plate Glass. Edward Ford did not intend that such a situation should arise in his own company. A statement he wrote in 1908 about his plans reflects this attitude. He said in part:

"One of my sons, John B., is operating the big Alkali Works at Wyandotte, Michigan, a family institution. My younger son, George R., is now the treasurer of the Plate Glass Company, starting in four years ago as assistant manager and later manager, after which I brought him into the office to learn the details of office work and to relieve me, as it is my intention soon to place him in full control."

Family control, as Mr. Ford had willed it, was well seated. His eldest son, John B., while actively in charge of the Alkali Works at Wyandotte, was vice president and a director of the Glass Works. He was 42. On the board at Rossford, too, was Edward Ford's nephew,

Cutting wheat. Years after this photo was taken, the great warehouse arose right near this spot, to the right.
In the picture, left to right: Lou Leamer, farmer who teamed during the early construction period at Edward Ford plant; Clarence Hubbell, and his father George. Orville, one of the Hubbell twins, is on the reaper, and Roger, son of George.
Photo taken about 1900. Most of the Hubbells later worked at Edward Ford Plate for many years.

Emory Leyden Ford of Wyandotte Alkali, now 32, son of Edward's brother, Emory, who had died in 1900; and Edward's youngest son, George, now 26.

The other board members were Attorney Fuller, Edward Ford's close friend and legal advisor; paymaster Joe Henry, an oldtimer with the Fords, and Claude Lewis, first a bookkeeper at Rossford, then plant superintendent and later sales manager.

Edward was a happy man, Everything was progressing better than he had dared to hope. In reply to a newspaper request for his biography, Mr. Ford complied briefly with his personal background, and then with obvious pride, wrote of his Rossford operation as follows:

"And now I must tell you something about this wonderful plant. The buildings occupy a space of about 15 acres, all closely connected. In the casting department are seven large 20-pot furnaces, six of which are in operation, one being held in reserve for emergencies.

"Producer gas is used for fuel, requiring eleven gas producers to furnish sufficient gas to operate the six furnaces. Adjoining this department is the lehr for annealing the plates, and next comes the grinding room in which are located 25 grinding machines. Adjoining this room is the polishing department containing 18 polishing machines.

"All of the machines are operated by electric motors, each ranging in horse power from 175 to 225. The Power House is next, in which are located four 1500 horsepower condensing engines, only three of which are necessary to generate electric current for all machinery and pumps throughout the plant.

"To give a full detail description of this plant would take up too much of your time in reading, so I will close by saying that the plant has been most successful from the start and closed the year 1907, with the largest output and sales in its history."

From a few hundred thousand feet of finished plate glass annually, the first decade saw production move up to 6,000,000 square feet per year.

Largest shipments at that time were going to Boston, New York and Chicago, but business was widening like waves from a stone tossed into placid water. There were Boston Plate & Window Glass; Ben Griffin of New York, close friend of Edward Ford; Semon-Bache of New York; William Glenny Glass of Cincinnati; the Binswangers; Hadley-Dean of St. Louis; another close friend,

Andrew Dole of Hooker Paint & Glass, Chicago; F. J. Coolidge and Sons of Atlanta, Ga.; Sharp Partridge Company of Chicago.

As 1910 approached, Edward Ford had good reason to feel happy about that first decade at Rossford. The plant was prospering. The payroll was expanding as more and more workers came in, and the town began spreading out.

His two eldest children, Mary and John, had families at Wyandotte. Mary, who had married Mark Reeves Bacon, had two sons, John B. F. Bacon and Milton Edward Bacon. John B. had two sons, John B., II and Fred, 11 and 13 respectively.

In Toledo, Laura Ford MacNichol, his first child by his second marriage, had four youngsters, Edward, Archibald, George P., Jr. and Laura.

Mrs. MacNichol's sister, Edna Ford, had married William W. Knight in 1904. They now had three boys, W. W. Jr., Milton and Edward. (Sam B. Knight and Elizabeth Ross Knight came later.)

And now Mr. Ford's youngest, George Ross Ford, had brought home a bride, Grace Miller, from Detroit. They were married February 22, 1907, and by late 1910, they had a son and daughter, George Ross Ford, Jr., and Grace Miller Ford. (Daughter Felia was born later.)

Edward Ford's five children were all living, and each was raising a family. His first grandchild, John B. F. Bacon, had been born in 1891. Now Mr. Ford had 13 grandchildren.

Grace Miller of Detroit became the bride of George Ross Ford in 1907. When she loaned this picture, she looked at it for a long moment, then chuckled: "My gracious—look at that head of hair."

CHAPTER 8

Expansion Keynotes Second Decade

Expansion in several ways marked the start of the second decade of the Edward Ford Plate Glass Company. At the first board meeting in January, 1910, the number of officers was increased from five to seven, lifting the general manager and general sales agent to the rank of officers.

This move affected Claude L. Lewis, already secretary of the company, and George W. DeMaid, in charge of sales. Lewis was elected to the board of directors, now consisting of Edward Ford, John B. Ford and George R. Ford, eldest and youngest sons of Edward, Rathbun Fuller and Lewis. Mr. DeMaid was elected secretary.

Preliminary discussions also were held at this meeting to consider increasing the monthly output of plate glass by 80,000 to 100,000 square feet. It was estimated that such an expansion would cost $150,000.

Twenty more acres of river frontage was acquired this year, ten of which were purchased from Hilrey C. Napier, the remainder from Stella Addison, John W. Gates and a Mr. Slavin. President Ford paid $17,767.70 for the land.

Death of George DeMaid caused Secretary Lewis to be made sales agent, and the appointment of Edmund Brown as general manager of the company to relieve Lewis of his factory production responsibilities.

This was voted at a board meeting in January, 1912, when the office of assistant secretary also was created. D. E. (Cy) Taylor was elected to this post.

Capital stock of the company was increased from $2,000,000 to $4,000,000 the following November.

By now the list of shareholders had increased from less than 10 to 23 persons, representing the company's 20,000 shares. This first large capitalization of the

Look at that smile of satisfaction on Edward Ford's face. His grandson, George R. Ford, Jr., now a member of the board of directors, clutches one of grandpa's favorite big black cigars.

Edward Ford Company was voted unanimously by the following shareholders:

Edward Ford	18,222 shares
George R. Ford	266 "
Claude L. Lewis	20 "
Rathbun Fuller	1 share
Carrie J. Ford	74 shares
J. B. Ford	17 "
Edna Ford Knight	16 "
Mary F. Bacon	130 "
George P. MacNichol	10 "
*Laura A. Ross	31 "
E. L. Ford	525 "
**Stella D. Ford	125 "
**Nell Ford Torrey	125 "
**Hettie B. Speck	125 "
***Mrs. A. MacNichol	2 "
****Elizabeth A. Malotte	16 "
J. M. Griffith	75 "
Jos. J. Griffith	30 "
C. E. Husted	50 "
*****Delilah Henry	70 "
Lillian Hurd	30 "
R. H. Pfieffer	30 "
Margaret H. Davis	10 "
TOTAL	20,000 shares

*Mother of Mrs. Edward Ford.
**Daughters of Emory Ford (Brother of Edward).
***Mother of G. P. MacNichol, Sr.
****Long-time friend and companion of Capt. Ford's wife, and Capt. Ford's housekeeper until his death.
*****Wife of Joseph Henry.

This significant milestone in the affairs of Edward Ford Plate almost seemed to symbolize the song just then the rage, Carrie Jacob Bond's "The End of a Perfect Day," written in 1910.

Nora Bayes was starring in the Follies; Marie Dressler convulsed them with "Heaven Will Protect the Working Girl," and the willowy Ruth St. Denis was making dancing history.

George Arliss . . . Otis Skinner . . . The three Barrymores . . . Raymond Hitchcock . . . George M. Cohan. They and many others kept the theaters filled . . . John Drew . . . James K. Hackett . . . Maxine Elliot . . . Anna Held.

And in Rossford, sheet music, player piano rolls and gramophone records filled almost every home as Rossfordians joined the nation in much shoulder and hip swaying in an era catapulted by Irving Berlin's introduction of "Alexander's Rag Time Band."

Mark Twain had just died. America stared heavenward, in city and prairie community, to see Halley's Comet. Roosevelt and Taft were at it hammer and tongs. Jack Johnson, the colored fighter, defeated Jim Jeffries. Amundsen reached the South Pole. Women were smoking cigarettes in public. Mary Baker Eddy died. Woodrow Wilson was governor of New Jersey. Prohibition was startling many, having just captured Indiana in its state-by-state creep. John D. Rockefeller was abused by the newspapers and the South for his $1,000,000 offer to help fight hookworm. . . . Kaiser Wilhelm had a birthday, and Archduke Francis Ferdinand of Austria was assassinated—June 18, 1914.

(Continued Page 41)

Edward Ford's love of boats, ever since those days when he slipped by Confederate shore guns, continued through the years. The Laura (above) was built on the Allegheny river, named for his daughter. Earlier, he had built a smaller one in a large puddle on the Allegheny during a drought, but even in normal water stages, they couldn't float it into mid-stream. It became a joke among members of Mr. Ford's family and friends, but no one ever had the temerity to say anything to him about it. Mr. Ford climaxed his boating career on the Maumee with one of the most magnificent of yachts. This view (right) of the coal-burning yacht was taken at Georgian Bay on one of the many family cruises.

Back in the days when they used individual ladles for pouring raw batch into the pots. A few of the men: Far left, Joe Kurrinick; fourth, Joe Liedigk; sixth, Bill Clover; kneeling, Fritz Rubley and Frank Saricke.

Can you identify these lads? Here's a tip—front row, third from left is Matt Pepper, Jr.

One of the laying gangs, about 1903-4

Taken about 1905, this group includes Mr. Becker, Charles Cupp, George Denman, Ed King, Abe Smith, Martin Honselman, Frank Saracki, Walter King (big black hat); Cliff Bragg, one of the Liedigks, Bill Butler and Milton Campbell.

Casting hall in early days:
Left to right: Matt Pepper and Gus Berkiss; third unknown; Mr. Heindrich. Left center: Foreman Joe Smith; Walter King, skimmer; right, Bob Hunter, skimmer-teemer.
Above in crane operator's booth: Charles Cook. He used to read the Bible in his cage, became so intent the men below had to yell at him when it came time to move the casting pot after the molten glass had been poured upon the grinding table. His son, Robert, became a famous lecturer for the Moody Bible Institute of Chicago. After retiring, Charles Cook moved to Woods, Wisconsin.

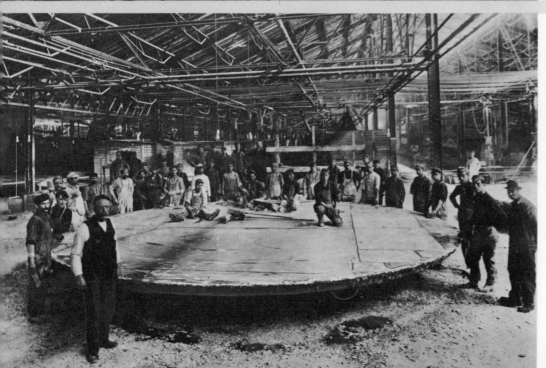

From the album of Roy Steward, this view shows the old No. 1 Grinding and Polishing shed. That's Vince Fildes, foreman, left, standing; some of the others at this 24-foot grinding table— William Weyrock, Emory Lorence, Arthur Brown, Karmen Juhas, Paul Heidrich, Irving Richards, Steve Kotowski and Fred Richards.

National interest was centered upon the headline, "Suffragists March on Capitol." Men grinned while ladies pored over the newspaper stories coming from the Women's National Medical Association convention in Indianapolis, marked by such headlines as "Hot Debate Over Corset."

Ladies of Rossford talked in whispers about the address given at the convention by an Ohio woman, Dr. Flora Smith of Newark, who had declared she "could not see why women thought it necessary to improve upon nature; neither she nor her mother had ever worn a corset."

The Aeolian Pianola was the rage, horses still hauled most of the people, including fire wagons and ambulances and the reapers in the vast wheat fields of Kansas; Buffalo Bill was the big Wild West show attraction, and the press was filled with photos captioned "Dynamic humanitarians," showing Booker T. Washington flanked by President William H. Taft and Andrew Carnegie.

It would be impossible to put labels on any single event as representative of America at the moment, but, industrially, Henry Ford captured the national spotlight with his announcement that he was going to raise his employees to $5.00 per day. Everybody speculated as to why Ford would pay such wages to men he could get for $2.00.

On April 5, 1915, Clark Husted, who had joined the company nine years before as traffic manager, was elected to the Board of Directors at Rossford. He also was elected secretary to replace Claude Lewis, resigned. Husted was now 35. Lewis' other position, general sales agent, was filled by H. J. Eckenrode.

Wilson was president now. The Marines had taken Vera Cruz. Most people were reading Booth Tarkington, Ida M. Tarbell, Edith Wharton, John Galsworthy, Edna Ferber, Jack London and Winston Churchill's "Inside of the Cup."

The nickelodeons had added an illustrated song to two movies for five-cent admissions. Mary Pickford . . . Douglas Fairbanks . . . The Perils of Pauline . . . Jane Cowl . . . Laurette Taylor . . . Pauline Frederick . . . Grace George . . . Al Jolson . . . Billie Burke . . . Alice Joyce . . . J. Warren Kerrigan . . . Francis X. Bushman . . . Broncho Billy.

Not long after the promotion of Mr. Husted, another new member of the board was posted—W. W. Knight, who had married Edward Ford's daughter, Edna, and who now was an official of Bostwick-Braun, large wholesale hardware concern. He was 38 years old.

He was listed as a member of the board of directors of the glass works in January, 1916, and was elected as one of the three vice presidents. The other two were John B. Ford, Edward's eldest son, and George, his youngest and who also was now treasurer. At this time, too, Mr. Husted was a director, secretary and purchasing agent.

And into this picture came one of Rossford's most admired men—Edwin C. Bowers, Sr. He was a veteran Ford man, having been first hired by Capt. Ford at Creighton in 1889. At Rossford, he became general manager, replacing Edmund Brown at the latter's death. Mr. Bowers was immediately voted as an officer of the company.

The Ford Glass Works was booming. Even the faint rumblings of the Kaiser's war drums in Europe were dimmed by the ambitious and noisy rehearsals of a small orchestra made up of Rossford employees. The group played for local dances.

They yearned to blossom into a band, but needed a professional leader.

The situation came to a head on a circular settee surrounding a pillar in the lobby of Toledo's leading hotel of the time, the Secor. Two men were talking about the idea of a band for Rossford.

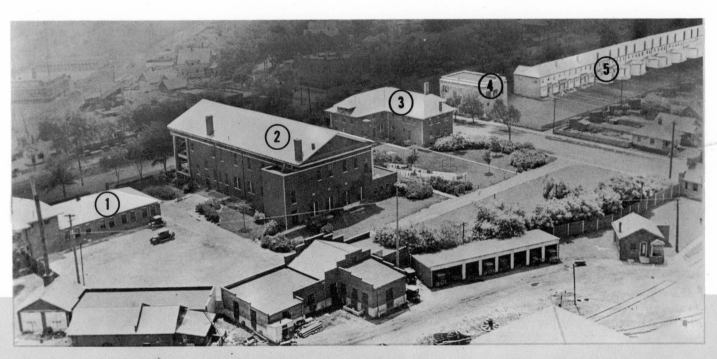

Taken from a water tower, this back view shows several interesting construction progress factors. At extreme left, (1) the office wing extension, still used and where Edward Ford's office was located; the Rossford Club (2) (completed in 1917), the old Rossford hotel (3) (since razed); the Rossford Savings bank, (4) where early Rossford baseball enthusiasts cavorted and the Terraces, (5) still occupied by Rossford employees and where several retired men and their families live.

"Well," one of them said, "I can see we need a leader for that. If we can find a professional musician who can do it—you'll have a band."

A tall man, thinking of quitting his job at the Overland, sat on the far side of the settee, drinking in the words. Music had been his life's blood. He was too bashful to introduce himself. From the hotel clerk he learned that one of them was George Ross Ford. He walked up to the mezzanine floor, scribbled a letter, sent it special delivery to Rossford.

Next day at work, the man was called at the Overland by his wife. Someone at Rossford had answered his letter, asking him to come over. A friend at Overland jumped into a car, drove the man to Rossford at once.

That's how Clarence H. Smith began. He met Cy Taylor, treasurer at the time. Taylor was excited when he heard that Smith had been with a circus band.

He related how the band had been organized only three months, that Henry Vanderkool was doing the best he could about leading the band, growing by leaps and bounds after its first "big" appearance. Smith wanted to know about that.

Learning that Mr. and Mrs. Edward Ford were visiting son George at his upriver home, band members voted to go to the Ford residence one afternoon. Under the trees on the big lawn, the odd assortment of non-uniformed bandsmen figuratively blew themselves into an enthusiastic collapse.

Edward Ford had never heard of the band. After the little concert was over, Mr. Ford came out on the lawn, asked many questions.

"Well, we need uniforms," he was told. "You'll get them," Mr. Ford replied, "what else?" "We need a director who is experienced with bands." Mr. Ford assured the man that one would be hired.

Mr. Ford, laughing now, asked "What else will you need?" He was told of the need for a suitable place to practice.

Mr. Ford didn't get a chance to reply. Mrs. Ford, who had edged close, broke into the conversation. "What you need is a club, a building where you can practice and—and—and, well, a club big enough for all those who want to do things."

That's how the fine brick Rossford Club House came into existence.

Mr. Smith stayed late at Rossford that day—holding a rehearsal that night in the Town Hall. George Ross Ford and Cy Taylor attended. Both were highly pleased.

When it came to salary, George Ford said, "Well, father will have to decide that." Next day Smith faced Edward Ford, who asked him to name his price. Smith did.

Mr. Ford's jaw dropped a little, Smith recalls. And he well remembers the reply of Mr. Ford. "Why, hell— that's more than anybody here gets."

"All right, you name the salary," Smith suggested. Mr. Ford did. Smith accepted, then added a remark that brought a large smile to President Ford's face. "If I am merely to direct the band, Mr. Ford, I'll have a lot of time on my hands. Maybe there's something else I could do."

Mr. Ford stood up, leaned across his desk and extended his hand to Smith. "We can use men like you," he smiled. Band leader Smith was given a personnel job, including the reading of meters in the Ford-owned houses occupied by Ford employees.

In the midst of all this, the fine production records being set in the factory, the splendid feeling between management and employees, the continued growth of Rossford came sinister headlines.

Ford Band—With Director Smith

Ford Band

Germany invaded Belgium. The American government gave the German ambassador his passports. A shocked United States went into action . . . World War I got under way on that fateful April 6, 1917.

War began to drain the ranks of Rossford. Orders for plate glass began to drop. Men had to be laid off.

Edward Ford's step was slower. He appeared at the office less and less. He was in his mid-70's.

There are many still living in Rossford who remember seeing the venerable plate glass manufacturer walking into groceries, meat markets, the drug store. No one knew why at the time.

Edward Ford was paying up long-overdue grocery bills of employees; he made arrangements that charge accounts should be continued for groceries, meats and medicine.

Plans had been given up to improve and re-open old Plant No. 1. Times were difficult now, but Edward Ford built larger wareroom quarters that he might keep most of his men at work.

And there was that day in the little second-floor dining room over the offices when every voice was hushed as Edward Ford looked across the table at his two guests, Henry Ford and his son, Edsel. Henry Ford had just made an offer for the Glass Works.

"Mr. Ford, you have made a most generous offer, and especially in these trying times . . . but I promised my father long ago that I would never sell this plant, that I would always keep it operating, one way or another . . . that our people, many of whom worked for my father, would always have a place here to earn their living, to raise their families."

Edward Ford presided, as he had at every board meeting in 20 years, at a brief session on June 21, 1919. It was Mr. Ford's final meeting as chairman of a board meeting.

Most of his time thereafter was spent at his home on Collingwood avenue at Bancroft street, where he had built a beautiful residence at the turn of the century.

About this time the city was jammed with celebrities and famous figures of the sporting world, along with such notables of the typewriter as Damon Runyan, Irving S. Cobb and Ring Lardner. Heavyweight Champion Jess Willard and youthful challenger Jack Dempsey would meet in the vast wooden bowl in Bay View Park under a blistering sun within days now.

Every newspaper in America and in many foreign countries were carrying stories daily about Toledo's great boxing contest, but Edward Ford, within four years of his 80th birthday, gave little thought to all this. He did smile, however, at his son's enthusiastic account of plans in Rossford for a great outdoor boxing show the night of July 3, to take advantage of the sporting crowds soon to invade Toledo.

He listened closely, but asked many questions about plans for the Glass Works.

The following December, at the board's final meeting of the year and decade, several decisions were made. It was a long session, a portentous meeting.

Board membership, originally five men, was increased from seven to nine men. This added Mr. Eckenrode, sales manager, and Edward F. MacNichol, one of the three sons of Laura Ford MacNichol. Edward, now 24, was the eldest. Archibald Ford MacNichol was 23 and his brother, George P. MacNichol, Jr., was 20, a student at Yale.

At this meeting, too, the Board reversed its previous decision about old Plant No. 1 and voted $200,000 for putting it into shape for reopening after several years of idleness.

PLANT EXTERIORS

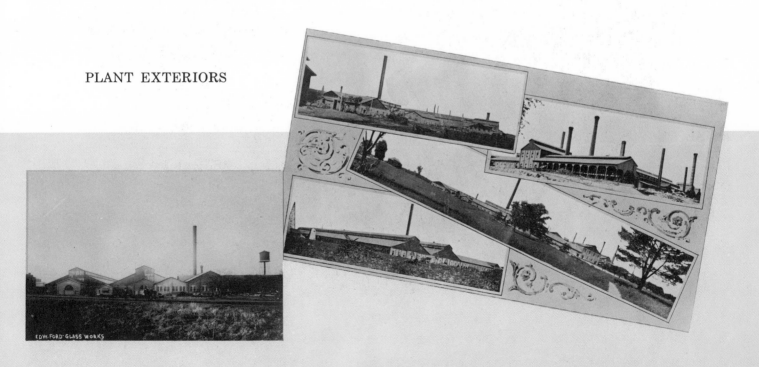

Bryan Post Card Company, Bryan, Ohio, made a post card view of Edward Ford Plate in 1903 when such cards were "the rage." These views were used to help create the over-all sketch of the old plant shown on pages 24 and 25.

GEORGE ROSS FORD

1882—1938

CHAPTER 9

The Roaring Twenties

What an era! The end of World War I ushered in a whole new concept of living. Prohibition had spawned new characters—bootleggers, rum runners, gangsters . . . machine guns carried in violin cases.

Jack Dempsey. Tex Rickard. Million-dollar gates. Talking movies. Babe Ruth. Bobby Jones. Valentino. Crystal radio sets . . . ("please stand by for two minutes") . . . Lindbergh's flight to Paris.

Meantime, in this world of swirling, booming, sky-rocketing happy madness, the stillness of death crept in upon the Rossford scene.

Edward Ford died at 8:15 p.m. on Thursday, June 24, 1920.

The dark-eyed little boy from Greenville, Indiana, had come a long, long way . . . 77 years.

Now his son, George Ross Ford, would carry on. Well, this man at 38, had tradition back of him. When he was nine years old, his little fist had held the silken cord that would unveil the great statue of his grandpa.

George was 21 when his grandfather died. And he had wept. He had loved the Old Lion, and had admired him greatly. He could well recall when the Old Captain held him on his knee, a big fat watch to his ear to hear it tick. He had taught George to tell time. And then he had given him a watch for his very own.

George Ross Ford must have drawn a long, deep breath. As the new president of the Edward Ford Plate Glass Company, he knew he had a vast responsibility. But he knew, too, that he had shrewd associates around him. Here was the management picture as he took over:

George R. Ford . . . President and Treasurer
John B. Ford . . . . . First Vice President
W. W. Knight . . . . Second Vice President
C. E. Husted . . . . . Third Vice President and Secretary
C. E. Taylor . . . . . Assistant Treasurer
E. C. Bowers . . . . . Manager
H. J. Eckenrode . . General Sales Agent

Half-brother John B. lived in Detroit, of course, still active head of Michigan Alkali, and his brother-in-law, Mr. Knight, was immersed in the affairs of big Bostwick-Braun, but both men kept in close touch with Rossford operations.

Clark Husted, his close friend, was an able executive at the plant, and Ed Bowers, an old-time plate glass man now, was general manager. Then, too, there was his father's great friend, Rathbun Fuller, and little John Griffith, who had been with the Fords since the Creighton days. He was actively connected with the Wyandotte alkali operations, but was in Rossford often on the business side of things, an expert in figures.

None were more aware than these men that times were changing rapidly. Mass production was now more than a trend; the automobile was coming into its own, with vast market potentials. New inventions were rapidly changing modes of living.

Competition in industry was keener than ever before, and particularly in the plate glass industry.

The Rossford management group agreed that new blood was needed, new faces . . . plant and equipment improvements that would require trained engineering skills.

And so in that first year of the fateful third decade, shortly after Edward Ford's death, David H. Goodwillie came upon the scene as chief engineer. He was then 33.

A graduate in mechanical engineering at Cornell in 1908, Mr. Goodwillie, after a year with American Steel & Wire Company, came to Toledo in 1909 to take charge of the city's new filtration plant. He became superintendent of the waterworks system in 1912, and in 1916 he was named Service Director of Toledo.

It was while serving on the city's board to evaluate the transit system as the basis for a new franchise ordinance that his ability as an engineer attracted the attention of Mr. Knight. Following a meeting with George and John B. Ford, and Mr. Knight, the young engineer was put in charge of engineering at Rossford.

A whole parade of improvements began to develop under his engineering leadership.

Before the year 1920 ended, George P. MacNichol, Jr. was elected assistant treasurer, and became full-time treasurer less than three months later, and a member of the board of directors.

Mr. MacNichol, who had played center on one of Scott High School's famous football teams, joined the glass works after leaving Yale. (His father had graduated from Harvard with a doctor's degree, and had married Edward Ford's daughter, Laura, in Creighton, in 1894.)

With college days past and interesting work ahead, Mr. MacNichol soon married. He met his bride-to-be, Emma Hetherington Smith, at the wedding of a mutual friend in Chicago.

Miss Smith was living in Norfolk, Virginia, at the time, but Toledo was not new to her. Although born in Atchison, Kansas, her parents had left soon after for Toledo, where her father, Roland K. Smith, became associated successively with the Ann Arbor and the Detroit, Toledo & Ironton railroads. Later the family moved to Hattiesburg, Mississippi, where Mr. Smith became president of the Mississippi Central Railroad. Later he moved to Norfolk to enter the lumber business.

Mr. MacNichol and Miss Smith were married November 23, 1922, in Norfolk. He was 23, his bride three months younger.

In December of that year, the board of directors voted to increase the company's capitalization from $4,000,000 to $10,000,000.

New blood, new faces, new skills . . . greatest capitalization in the company's history. But before we go further, let's look back at some of the scenes, some of the faces that had helped to bring Edward Ford Plate up to this point.

David H. Goodwillie

HENRY WERNER, JR.

Few know Henry in Rossford without recalling the way he entered the community's activities. Rossford Savings Bank was founded by Edward Ford and George Ross Ford, Sr. Many benefits to Rossfordians resulted.

The operating cashier died suddenly in 1920. Mr. Ford called the old National Bank for a temporary replacement. Mr. Werner was sent over "for a few days." Henry has been in charge for 36 years. Meantime, he has headed many civic groups, including 22 years as president of Rossford's Board of Education, and Flower Hospital's Board of Trustees.

CHAPTER **10**

Rossford Personalities

There are men working at Rossford whose family background goes far back into Fordiana—back to New Albany in the days of Capt. Ford.

A fascinating example is the King family.

William H. King, who died in Rossford in 1912, was a close friend and employee of Capt. Ford. Born in Salem, Indiana, in 1830, he moved to nearby New Albany and for a time operated a feed store. That's when he first became acquainted with Capt. Ford.

When the Old Lion went broke, after succeeding in making plate glass at New Albany, Bill King was one of those who rallied round, and loaned money to the Captain. Later, when Capt. Ford went East to try a comeback, Bill King began working for Edward Ford at Jeffersonville.

When this venture collapsed about 1879, King began farming part of a 1,000-acre tract purchased from the government by his father, Samson.

Samson had dug a 65-foot well for his contemplated house. To his consternation, the water was unfit for drinking.

Puzzled, he took a sample to Dr. Elijah Newland of New Albany. (Dr. Newland had married a daughter of Washington C. DePauw, cousin of Capt. Ford. DePauw, a banker, investor and one of Indiana's most powerful behind-the-throne politicians of the time, had taken over Capt. Ford's glass works at New Albany.)

After testing the sample of water, Dr. Newland looked at Samson and said: "Why Sam, you have a gold mine here." Together they went to Indianapolis where a laboratory reported the water contained 995 different kinds of minerals. Years later, son William built a 120-room health resort hotel, and formed the Samson King

Mineral Well Company in 1886. Guests came from as far away as Louisville, Cincinnati and Columbus, Ohio.

Then Edward Ford wrote to King, asking him to come on to work at Ford City. King couldn't resist.

He put the hotel and all property up for sale, and left for Ford City in 1892. The resort was abandoned, finally disappeared. It was located about four miles west of Memphis, Indiana, 25 miles north of Jeffersonville.

Mr. and Mrs. William King, who gave a full deck of Kings to the Fords, Capt. and Edward.

A son, Walter O. King, 1006 Kelsey avenue, Toledo, shook his head in recalling this, and smiled: "Father was doing fine with the resort, but he went to Ford City as a casting hall foreman at $125 a month."

* * * *

William King not only gave up a good business to rejoin the Fords, but he gave to the Fords six sons. Those sons in turn had sons who still work at Rossford.

The six sons were Henry, Charles, Edward, William Jr., John and Walter. Let's spend a moment with each.

Henry—B, 1856; died 1930. Worked in Ford's Jeffersonville plant. Henry's son, James, works in the Rossford powerhouse; another son, Walter, who once worked in Rossford carpenter shop, became a Chicago banker.

Charles—Worked in Jeffersonville and Ford City. Born in Jeffersonville, 1861; died in Ford City. He was a grinder.

Edward—Followed glass works from Jeffersonville to Creighton. Worked for Fords 64 years.

William, Jr.—Born 1873; died 1928, Rossford. Started in casting hall at Ford City, 1893; came to Rossford in 1898. Son, Lester, works in Twin Grinder plant at Rossford.

John—Born 1875. Began in casting hall at Ford City. Came on to Rossford, where he died in 1929.

Walter—Born 1879, in Jeffersonville. He began as waterboy at Ford City when he was 16. Such boys used wooden shoulder yokes to carry two pails of water. When another lad, Albert Campbell, while carrying water, walked smack into a light of large plate glass and broke it, Walter got his job.

William Patton, Walter's school teacher, tried to get Superintendent Matt Pepper to fire Walter so he could return to school. Pepper refused. This was just before Christmas, 1896 . . . The following summer, a casting hall man collapsed from the heat, and Walter got his job— a raise from $1.20 per day to $1.80 per day.

Mr. King recalls that casting hall men in those days drew and cast 20 pots and then went home. This job required from six to twelve hours. The men worked six days per week.

When the first lehr was built at Ford City, Walter was made a skimmer, getting $2.20 per day to cut and skim. Then he became a skimmer-teemer at $3.00 per day.

Walter came on from Ford City while the Rossford plant was being built, going back to $1.20 per day as a day laborer, but came up to $1.80 per day again when the new casting hall opened. In 1911, Walter became a casting hall boss.

One day one of his men made a mistake, pushing a plate back atop another, ruining both plates. Superintendent Harry Cochran, who had replaced Matt Pepper, ordered King to fire the man. King refused, explaining that the man would not make such a mistake again. Cochran came back in the afternoon, again demanding that King fire the man.

King quit. He went to Detroit where he obtained a position as a conductor on the Detroit, Monroe and Toledo interurban line. He remained until the line was abandoned in 1932.

* * * *

William H. King, father of those six men, had two brothers-in-law who worked for the Fords. One of them, Clark Gregg, loaned money to Capt. Ford after he had to give up his glass works in New Albany. Gregg had been a window glass blower for Capt. Ford and, earlier, had worked on one of Mr. Ford's boats.

William Gregg, brother of Clark, really got close to the Fords. His mother, Sally, for a time gave one breast to infant William and the other to Edward's infant brother, Emory. (The Greggs for a time lived in Greenville, where Edward and Emory were born. Capt. Ford's wife was 40 when Emory was born.)

William Gregg worked as an accountant at Ford City. After the unveiling of the statue of Capt. Ford in Ford City in 1891, Gregg buried a fruit jar nearby. It contained one of the speeches made at the unveiling.

James King, son of Henry — one of those original six King boys whose father, William, sold his Indiana health resort to join Capt. Ford at Ford City. Not only was he the oldest active employee at 70, but he began at Rossford when the Glass Works opened in 1899. Born in Jeffersonville, Indiana, he went to the Allegheny Valley with his father to rejoin the Fords, his uncles already

The gay '90's. , The four-horse surrey, with the fringe on top, a rented vehicle for young blades to attend a picnic, dance, halloween party or go skating, was taken in front of Joe Smith's home on Third Avenue in Ford City about 1896. Many of the lads and lassies came on to Rossford. Can you identify any of them?

on the job there at Creighton, Tarentum and Ford City.

Although he was only six years old at the time, when his father worked in the Ford City plant, Jim recalled that in the panic of 1892, Capt. Ford nailed up all the windows in the Ford City plant—doing much of the work himself in his anger against the low state of the protective tariff at the time.

(The Old Lion was 81 at the time, about one year after the statue had been unveiled in his honor.)

* * * *

Joe Smith. Now there's a common name. But the Joseph Smith who is subject of this part of the Rossford scene was a most uncommon Joe Smith.

Born in England, July 4, 1846, Joe Smith was working at the famous Pilkington Glass Works in England when he received a letter from Capt. Ford. Joe arrived in Creighton not long after that to join the growing number of skilled plate glass men the Old Lion was pulling together.

Joe Smith was father of 14 children—seven boys and seven girls. And most of them figured in Fordiana in one way or another, some of the Smith girls from England marrying some of the King boys from New Albany and Jeffersonville. Father Joe came on to Rossford and was one of the three pre-1900 casting hall foremen—Jeff Venable and John King (one of the six King boys) being the other two.

James, William, and Abe, all born in England, worked at Creighton, Ford City, Tarentum and Rossford. Joseph, Jr., last of the Smith boys born in England (1882), worked in Rossford for many years. He died in 1930.

John, born in Tarentum, 1886, worked at Rossford's grinding and polishing department for many years, too. He died in 1953.

Tom, born in 1890, began in the pot house at Rossford in 1907. He left in 1924, but returned in 1928 and completed 17 years as an electrician.

Mary, born in England, married William King, Jr. (one of the six King boys) in Ford City. Her sister, Ellen, married another of the King boys, Jim, in 1908. Jane, born in Creighton, married Frank Hamel of Rossford.

Margaret, also born in England, married Charles Metzler, a Rossford kiln dresser.

Alice, born in England, arrived with the family in Creighton when she was six years old. She came on to

Rossford with the family and in 1907 married Fred Littek, a Ford potmaker who was born in Germany. The other three children died in infancy.

* * * *

It was a blistering July noon. Some of the factory and office men were, as usual, playing baseball. Clark Husted took off his dripping white shirt, hung it on a nearby tree to dry out, hustled back to the playing field.

In the excitement of the game no one seemed to notice that George Ford, Sr., having watched Clark spread his shirt carefully along a limb, walked rapidly into the Club house, returned shortly with his hands behind his back, maneuvering toward the tree where Husted's shirt was drying.

When the factory whistle blew everybody rushed away. Husted grabbed at his shirt on the run, was brought up sharply when the shirt refused to accompany him. Clark tugged impatiently a few times, then squinted, looking closer. Both arms and the collar had been nailed to the limb.

Husted walked hurriedly to the office. Saying nothing to anybody, he called a Toledo department store, ordered 12 white shirts and gave instructions to have them sent to his office at Edward Ford Plate. After making sure the sizes given were for his own body, he said: "And charge those to George Ross Ford."

* * * *

Robert L. Enis. Native of Whitehouse, Ohio, Bob came to Toledo as a youth; delivered groceries for Fred Summerfield, 730 Lorain street, across the river from the new Ford plant. That was in 1900.

Bob used to stare across the water, thinking how he'd like to work there. That mysterious place fascinated him. One day he rented a boat from Slaven's boathouse at the foot of Hickory street. He rowed across, climbed the high bank and sought out Paymaster Joe Henry. He got a job.

As the years rolled on, Bob Enis worked at practically every job in the factory. He was in charge of employment at one time, had charge of rentals of the Ford-owned houses and the many attendant duties; as "property protection" became a factor, he was placed in charge of

Robert L. Enis

company patrolmen—or plant protection personnel as they are now called.

He used to take $50,000 in cash (the insurance limit on payrolls at the time) to the factory from a Toledo bank, making two trips. On some trips, a Toledo city patrolman was assigned to him. Once a city patrolman, waiting for Bob in the bank, rested the end of his gun barrel (a sawed-off shotgun) on the toe of his right shoe.

The gun went off, taking part of the patrolman's foot with it. That patrolman for years operated one of the elevators in the East Side Police Station.

Physically, Bob is not a large man, but he was a colorful thread in the skeins that went into the pattern of Rossford sports activities. Sometimes he played; sometimes he managed. He and Vern Evans used to stage some great horse-shoe competition, and Bob's hilarious "catsup knockout" punch in the Rossford club ring, described elsewhere in this book, made local history.

Everybody knew Bob. He retired in 1938, after more than three decades of service.

* * * *

Samuel Frautschi, who clerked in several Toledo department stores before crossing the river to become one of Rossford's pioneer merchants, had four sons—Fred, the eldest, who died during World War I flu epidemic; Arnold, Walter and Herman.

Some of the things Walter recalls: his first automobile ride with Dr. Elmer Holst. They crossed the river for a spin in Toledo's downtown in the gray no-top Maxwell. Right down Madison avenue they rolled. Walter, about 15 then, hung on to his hat desperately, Dr. Holst cussing nervously as he was blinded by approaching lights of a few other cars on the thoroughfare. Walter recalls how Dr. Holst got out and lit the carbide lights with a long match. . . . Oscar Holst, brother of Dr. Holst. Oscar's wife, Jennie, was an expert with the needle. She did much of the "fine sewing" for the Fords . . . the thousands of "Dayton Laying-Gang" shoes sold to Ford workers— all leather, very heavy and with half-inch soles . . . the Last Chance Saloon, right on the line of the south boundary of the town. Run by Jules Mathis . . . "everybody" in Rossford went to Billy Wiel's on Saturday night. Billy's place was on Superior street, between Bergen and Bacon . . . tavern and bowling alley on the first floor, big dance floor upstairs, reached by an outside stairway. They danced to the fiddle of Frank Krakau and the cornet of Hubert Vanderkool. George Purcell played the piano sometimes. . . . Frautschi's covered wagon, almost like the old Conestoga trail wagons . . . wagon had a 12-foot box. And Sam stretched a big canvas top over hoops. He solicited orders in this wagon, and delivered them in it. . . . Walter recalls six members of what he believes to be Rossford's first baseball team—catcher Hopkins, pitcher Skinny Campbell, first baseman Bill King, second baseman Walter Brown, rightfielder Otis Warner and center-

Van Hudepohl, office worker who joined Fords in Creighton, and began in the Edward Ford plant at Rossford in its first year.

fielder Dr. MacNichol (father of George P. MacNichol, Jr.) Dr. MacNichol didn't play much, Walter recalls, but encouraged the others to play. He rooted for both teams.

* * * *

Sylvanus S. Hudepohl. Everybody knew him as Van.

Born in Allegheny City (now a part of Pittsburgh) in 1857, Van became an office clerk for Edward Ford in Creighton when the latter was president of Pittsburgh Plate Glass Company.

Van and his family came on from Creighton, landing in Toledo, October 9, 1899, just as the Ford Works in Rossford was getting under way. His daughter, Ethel May, was seven years old. When she was 21, she began teaching school in Rossford, from 1913 until about 1915, when she married Hugh MacPhie.

Mrs. MacPhie is proud of the fact that Mrs. Edward Ford made it possible for her to take a course in an art school. (She paid her back, too.)

Van Hudepohl was 25 when George Ross Ford was born in Creighton, and watched him grow to manhood. The two became close friends, and developed the habit of exchanging humorous birthday postcards.

Van died four days before his 81st birthday. Beside his bed was a new birthday card, from George Ross Ford . . . and George Ford died a few weeks later, too!

* * * *

Henry J. Beuth, one of Rossford's pioneer stalwarts. He's been called Whitey ever since he was a little boy, when his father worked for the Fords in Creighton. (The Germans there called him "Weiser" or "Schummel," meaning white or whitey, due to his very blond hair.)

Whitey's father, Peter Joseph, joined the Fords in Creighton in 1889, coming from Stolberg, Germany, near Aachen, where he had worked as a plate glass polisher.

Whitey's mother, Mary, who died in Rossford Novem-

(On the left): Peter Joseph Beuth. Born in Germany where he worked in glass. Joseph had a long career with the Fords, first at Creighton, and on to Rossford.

(On the right): Whitey Beuth, long time crane operator at Rossford. Retired, he is son of Peter Joseph.

ber 18, 1918, was known far and wide for her culinary ability. Whitey said that his mother, as a young girl, was sent from Germany to Belgium to learn French cooking by the Belgian owners of the German glass works near Aachen.

Whitey recalled that one of the proudest moments of his father's life came in 1897, when he won his citizenship papers at Creighton. He came to Rossford in 1907, working in the casting department.

Whitey started to work in the casting hall that same year, as a crane operator. (His father retired in 1931 and died July 4, 1941. He is buried in Springdale, Pennsylvania, a few miles from Creighton.)

Whitey was one of the many little boys who used to hurry across the old West Penn Railroad tracks at Creighton, carrying a well-filled dinner pail for his dad. In winter, the quart-size tops of those dinner pails carried hot soup, with the rest of the pail usually crammed with meat, hot potatoes and gravy, and a big wedge of pie. To insulate the food against the bitter cold, the women always wrapped the dinner pails in their shawls or "fascinators."

Whitey remembered Capt. Ford quite well, often seeing him making his daily trip to Pittsburgh, arriving at the station in a surrey drawn by two white horses.

"I will never forget the day that Mother had to be taken to a Pittsburgh hospital. She was taken down to the station in the undertaker's black hack.

"Quite a group had gathered. I saw Capt. Ford arrive. He stared at the crowd, hustled forward and wanted to know what the rumpus was all about. Despite his age (he was in his early 80's then) Capt. Ford elbowed his way through that crowd to Mother, and assisted her aboard the train.

"He stayed right with her, and in Pittsburgh he wouldn't leave until he was sure everything possible was being done for her.

"That," said Whitey, "was the Ford way of doing things."

Whitey knew Edward Ford quite well, of course, and always was a great admirer of George Ross Ford, Sr.

"Yes, I remember the Old Captain, and his son, Edward, and Edward's son, George Ross Ford, Sr. . . . but let me tell you something that to me is typical of the Ford family.

"I'll never forget the day young George (George, Sr.'s son) came into the casting hall to work. It was a hellish hot day, and, of course, the heat around those pot furnaces was awful. I asked him not to attempt to work in there, explaining that even the old-timers often keeled over. That young fellow insisted, however.

"He went home to lunch. I learned later that he collapsed on the kitchen floor of his home and just about scared the daylights out of his mother . . . and you know what? That young cuss came right back to the casting hall the next morning and stuck with it . . . I'll never forget that."

* * * *

William F. Fague. Bill began with Edward Ford Plate in 1921, becoming office manager and assistant treasurer.

Like Clark Husted, he came from a railroad traffic office, having worked under Clark's father, Giles, in the Lake Shore & Michigan Central office.

Born in Toledo in 1879, Bill attended old Central High. His parents moved to Iola, Kansas, where he got into the cement business, first as an accountant and later as sales and traffic manager, 1911 to 1917, when he went to Cuba with a cement concern, returning to Toledo in 1920.

Bill, a whizz with figures, coded Toledo's first fire alarm system. They used the bell in old Central High for it.

Oldtimers will recall his grandfather, John Faskin, a colonel in three different Northwestern Ohio regiments in the Civil War, and who organized the Burns Curling Club. People thronged the area at the foot of Jefferson street to watch the Burns members curl on the Maumee when that was one of Toledo's top sports.

* * * *

Grant Sarver. He got scared when Capt. Ford watched him cut glass. Eldest of 13 children, Grant was born on a farm near Sidney, Ohio, and began at Rossford before he was 16—in June of 1901.

A mason's helper under Gus Berkiss, Grant later worked for John Scharf, then into a series of mechanical jobs, winding up in the wareroom in 1903.

Veteran Grant Sarver

This was to be his work for many years. Inclined to self-effacement about his own abilities, Grant, once he had a good background in glass, would stand his ground when he felt he was right. When Claude Lewis, production manager at the time, informed Grant that a new wareroom superintendent was coming in, (Claude's brother, Roy Lewis) Grant got busy.

Grant felt that Roy, while a nice person, had no background in this phase of the business. And so Grant quit, taking a job in his brother's bakery. . . . A year later, Claude Lewis called Sarver back. He was given back his old job, chief inspector, and a bit later became warehouse superintendent, the position he felt he should have had before.

"I'll never forget the first time I saw old Cap Ford come into the wareroom. I had heard the men talk about him before. Many of the boys had worked for him in Pennsylvania.

"There was always a lot of yelling and general noise in the wareroom, but when the old Cap showed up everything grew quiet, sudden-like. I was cutting glass, but I was scared and tried to pay no attention. He kept coming closer and closer, shaking hands, greeting various men, watching their work.

"My hand shook so bad, I could hardly cut glass, as he came up. Finally I couldn't ignore him any more. He was standing right by me, watching me cut. I straightened up and glanced at him. He was staring at me. Gosh, I'll never forget his eyes. They bored right through me.

"Suddenly, he grinned at me—a real friendly smile. Then he walked on. I couldn't take my eyes off him for a time. He was a commanding figure. I began to understand why the men thought so much of him."

Early in his wareroom days, Grant got an idea how the big plates of glass, after leaving the grinding and polishing department, could be cleaned more easily and quickly. Pumice was smeared on the glass and allowed to dry, and then wiped off. Why not clean them with water and squeegee the water off at once?

Getting up sufficient courage to ask for an interview with Edward Ford, he got it easy enough and went into the president's office, standing in front of the big flat table until Mr. Ford turned away from his roll-top desk.

"SIT DOWN," Mr. Ford snapped.

"I sat down so hard that I thought the chair and I would both collapse," Grant recalls.

"Then he smiled, offered me one of his big black cigars. I told him I didn't smoke, and that pleased him. He listened attentively to my idea. Some time after that we were ordered to use the new method on small lights. Later, the big panes were cleaned the same way. Mr. Ford used to stop often after that and talk with me, asking me a lot of questions about the work."

Mr. Sarver retired as warehouse superintendent after 32 years with the company. Three of his four sons, Roger, Robert and James, work at Rossford.

* * * *

James H. Bayer. He used to carry the Ford payroll—all in gold and silver—around in a wheelbarrow, accompanied by Constable Charley Sutton, who looked all business with a shot-gun in his hand.

But we're getting ahead of our story. Jake Bayer, who retired after 43 years of service, is one of the best known of the oldtimers. Everybody, from Edward Ford right on through the ranks, liked Jake.

Born in Tarentum, Pennsylvania, where his father, John, had arrived from Stolberg, Germany, as an expert grinder, Jake Bayer was only two years old when Capt. Ford's statue was unveiled.

Jake Bayer

When Jake began working at Rossford in 1912, he was 23 and plate glass plants weren't new to him. His father, after working at Tarentum, moved to Alexandria, Indiana, where Jake first worked in the Pan-American Plate plant, once owned by Capt. Ford's cousin, Wash DePauw, but taken over later by Pittsburgh Plate Glass. He became a booker and matcher, the job he first had at Rossford. A co-worker was Verne Evans; their boss, George Saelzer.

Jake became paymaster and timekeeper about 1915, replacing the aging Joe Henry, who had been with the Fords for so long. Edward Ford also put Jake in charge of the Ford-owned houses, about 275 families occupying company-owned dwellings at that time. Bayer knew them all personally, and the names of every child; watched over their needs, particularly when work was slack.

"I used to tell Edward Ford about their problems. His answer was always the same. 'Take care of it,' he would say, 'but don't tell anybody about it.' In hard times, no Ford family ever got low on groceries, fuel or medicine just because cash was short. That's the way the Fords were. I know. I was close to that picture for years.

"Often I used my own judgment, when I couldn't reach Mr. Ford or George. They had given me my orders about such matters. 'Take care of it.' That's all they'd say."

Jake became famous around the plant for his ability to remember faces. There were about 1,700 men on the payrolls at the time. As they lined up and came to the window, Jake would merely look at the man, and hand him the cash due him, deductions for an advance or extra money for some special job the man had done, all figured ahead of time by Jake.

Often he went into the plant and stuffed pay into the man's pocket if his hands were too dirty to handle the money as he stood beside a grinding table or in some other department.

Dave Goodwillie came upon a strange scene one payday in the early 20's. The "boys" had got to betting on Jake's ability to pay the right amount to the right man. They realized he knew all the faces, so when Jake said he could do it blindfolded, they took him up. Chief Engineer Goodwillie stared as he watched Jake paying off accurately, man after man.

Queried about it recently, Jake grinned as he said: "I could tell who it was by the sound of his voice . . . and I could recognize a man by the sound of his step. Every man walks differently, if you make a point of familiarizing yourself with it.

"Yes," Jake grinned when asked about carrying cash in a wheel-barrow, "in those days the Fords paid twice a month in gold and silver. The money was pretty heavy, of course, so I used a wheel-barrow to lug the pay from one department to another."

About 1929, Jake was put back into the factory, at the insistence of Mr. Goodwillie. He was made night superintendent. Four years later he became assistant superintendent, under Chester Henderson. The latter was replaced by the late Emory Durivage.

In 1936, while assistant to Durivage, Jake was promoted, placed in charge of the wareroom and packing department, the position he held when he retired in 1954.

John Scharf, a veteran from the 1898 days, recently commented upon Mr. Goodwillie insisting upon Jake Bayer returning to an important job in the plant.

"Mr. Goodwillie was impressed by Jake's way of handling his paymaster job. He knew Jake had something upstairs."

Mr. Bayer married Elsie Heidrich, daughter of Adolph of Rocky Ridge. Her brother, Jacob, a polisher, was a 50-year man at Rossford.

* * *

As a little boy he loved to play around the glistening piles of cullet at Edward Ford Plate, and in the great mountain of grinding sand. He loved, too, to watch the shiny grains of sand streaming from his tiny fist as he dug into the transplanted sand dunes.

Sands of time, almost, as the grains squirted from the bottom of his fist . . . sands of time, indeed. He progressed through grade school to the eighth grade at Rossford, thence to Waite in East Toledo, for Rossford had no high school then.

Doc, they called him . . . Doc Holst, for he was the son of Dr. Elmer Holst, Rossford's pioneer physician. That name clung through many years of the sands of time—through his newspaper writing career.

Then, more recently, he came to be known as Lord Lawrence, daily columnist. And the sands of time, still running through Doc's fist, brought him his greatest assignment, going to Monaco to cover Grace Kelly's wedding.

* * *

Ethel Enderbury started March, 1916. She came with a number of families from Valley Park, Missouri, where fire had destroyed the glass plant, followed by a devas-

tating flood. Her grandfather, James, had come from Pilkington Plate in England to join Capt. Ford at New Albany in the late 1860's as a kiln dresser.

Miss Enderbury's father, Thomas, born near Birmingham, England, started at Rossford in 1916, too.

She began in the office under Cy Taylor. She used to help prepare Christmas baskets for the children of employees; recalls when management used to charter the City of Toledo steamer and take employees and the Ford band to Sugar Island.

Her sister, Frances, worked in the office, 1916 to 1929.

* * *

Florence Watters began in 1922. She had come to Rossford in 1914. Knew Grant Sarver. He suggested she apply for an office job. She handled production figures. During inventory period everybody jumped in to help, she says; recalls how Clark Husted always arrived first, grabbed the adding machine and kept it all day.

Remembers how Fague, when checking accounting sheets, would on occasion purposely call out the wrong number. When somebody caught it, he'd look up over his glasses and grin: 'Just seein' if you were listenin'.'

"Everything has changed greatly, of course," she says. "It used to be just like a family. Everybody always jumped in to help some other department in the office in an emergency. Why, some of us used to go upstairs to the kitchen and help the cook (a colored woman—Mrs. Davis—then) to get the food ready. We fried chicken— many things."

* * *

Mrs. Luella (Pringle) Hayes began 1923 in production figures, later into billing, with Miss Watters. Still at it.

Recalls how George Ford, Sr. always made the rounds to look at everybody's Valentine cards.

Her father, Calvin Pringle, worked for Bill Philbin, in charge of the labor gang. Many Pringles (her cousins and uncles) worked at Rossford prior to 1920.

* * *

Ardell Williams began in 1922. Her father, James M. Williams, began as bookkeeper in 1916. Came from Valley Park, Missouri; whole train load of families headed for Rossford.

Her father died suddenly after returning home from the first oldtime party held in 1949 in the Commodore Perry. She and her father were the only Father-Daughter combination at the party.

Ardell began working under Fague in 1924 in Workmen's Compensation Claims.

* * *

Joseph Mainz. He's one of the real oldtimers, and an authority on grinding and polishing methods used by Capt. Ford in the early days at Creighton.

Joe was born in 1879, in Gelsenkierchen, an industrial city of West Germany. His father, Bernard, a casting hall man in Germany, arrived in Creighton in 1886, about five years after the Creighton Works was estab-

These seven old timers represent 331 years with the Fords. Left to right are E. J. Durivage, Matt Kramer, all at the plant when it started; Harry Craver, John Baillet, who had 60 years service, having joined the plant in 1899; Joe Mainz, who also began in 1899, coming from Creighton; and James Bourbina.

lished. Joe had two brothers; John, the eldest, a casting hall man, and Bernard, Jr., a polisher who went into the grocery business in Tarentum, where he died in 1944.

At Creighton, Joe began as a rouge boy at 13, carrying pails of red polishing material to the bench of the machine to which he was assigned. His main job was to see that there was always plenty of polishing rouge at hand.

Coming to Rossford in 1899, when he was 20, Joe was among the first polishing men when the Edward Ford Works began operations that year. He says the "English polishers" used at Creighton by the Fords were square tables that carried 180 square feet of glass per table. The tables moved back and forth under round iron blocks faced with felt.

The glass was polished for eight hours on one side and then turned over for another eight-hour polishing session. Each shift of men worked 12 hours, so that only two foremen per 24 hours were needed.

He recalls some of the early foremen—Mr. Kapsteiner, who came from Germany, and who gave Capt. Ford some excellent batch ingredient tips; Joe Forst, who later went to the polishing department at the Ford City plant; Sam Emsweller; "Judge" Nicholas, a giant in stature; Ed King (one of the six King boys) first grinder foreman at Creighton who came on to Rossford where he became first grinding foreman; and Charles Kallis, an uncle of Joe Mainz. Kallis was one of the first casting hall men at Creighton. Capt. Ford persuaded him to come from Germany.

"Yes," Joe said in reply to a question, "sports were quite active even in the early days at Creighton. The Fords encouraged the men in that respect. Every department had a baseball team. Tarentum had a county semi-pro team made up largely of Ford employees."

They played football, too. Joe, small of stature himself, grinned in recollection.

"Some of those German fellows, who seemed to have two by four beams for shoulders, used to enjoy mauling each other more than they did in getting their hands on the football," he said.

He specifically recalls George Giles, unusually powerfully built and a wild man on the football field. He was killed in a casting hall accident at Creighton at the time he was superintendent of the department.

Giles' mother and Mrs. Artemus Pitcairn were sisters. (Artemus was a cousin of John Pitcairn, the man who gradually built up voting forces that resulted in Capt. Ford and his two sons severing relations with Pittsburgh Plate Glass.)

Mr. Mainz well remembers George Ross, father of Edward Ford's wife, Caroline. "He was a small man," says Joe, "and was yardmaster at Creighton. I never saw him get mad. He was pleasant at all times to everybody."

Bill Sim

Joe Mainz retired in 1950, completing 58 years with the Fords. His wife, Anna, was a Stricker girl, four days younger than Joe.

* * *

"Do I recall the unveiling of the statue to Capt. Ford? . . . Why hell, son—I own a piece of that statue."

His mind as quick, at the age of 88, as a snapping turtle's jaws, Bill Sim, who came from England in 1890 at the age of 22 to work at Ford City, kept a group of plate glass men on the edge of their chairs as he recalled the early days.

Bill, who sang in the choir of the Methodist Church on Third Avenue in Ford City (built with funds given by Capt. Ford's wife, he recalls), followed Edward Ford to Rossford in 1899.

He didn't stay long, grief stricken by the death of his two sons in Rossford within a year. He returned to Ford City in 1901, where his wife died that year in childbirth!

Born in England in 1868, Sims spent 12 years at Ford City, interrupted only by his short stay at Rossford, before moving on to other plants as the years rolled along.

He saw Capt. Ford only a few times. "What a tremendous character he was," said Bill shaking his head, "a commanding figure no one could ever forget." He chuckled softly as he recalled Ford City days.

"The day before Capt. Ford would come up the Valley for a visit to the Ford City Works, the word always got around quickly. A common expression on such an occasion was, 'Cap Ford's comin' tomorrow. Better be on your toes, boys.' "

At 88, Bill Sim was probably one of the very last survivors of those 3,000 workers who volunteered a day's wages to pay for the statue to Capt. Ford.

* * *

A long-time employee and native of the Rossford community is Irving Richards, 170 Hannum avenue, Rossford, who was born in nearby Eagle Point in 1884, when that area was mostly farm land.

He went to work at the Ford plant when he was 18 (1902). He became a boss car man, shuttling the grinding tables, and later joining the machine group, whose members installed new machinery, repaired heavy equipment and generally took over in break-down emergencies.

Irving, small of stature, became boss of the "Bull Gang"; likes to recall two instances of his Bull Gang days.

Once a lehr broke down, due to over-heated rods. Repairing such a job usually required several days. Told that each of his men would be given a day off if the lehr was repaired by midnight, Gang Boss Richards hurried across the street and purchased 18 pairs of heavy gloves for the blistering task ahead.

Richards had the lehr ready by midnight, a super-human performance. The men got their days off, and the company paid Irving for the gloves.

He likes to recall an experience with the late David H. Goodwillie.

"Sometimes things were quiet," Irving recalls, "and the gang would just idle around. When they would see Mr. Goodwillie coming, they'd just fade away." Irving stopped at this point to laugh uproariously.

"One day," he said, "some of the men were sitting on a big rack of glass in the wareroom. They saw Goodwillie coming. They slipped around to the other side of the rack.

"Dave had seen 'em. He came up close to the rack and quietly slipped to one end, and peeked around the other side, right into the face of one of the Bull Gang. That guy wanted to run, but it was too late.

"Goodwillie stared hard at him for a moment, then grinned, as he said: 'Don't ever slip away like that. It looks bad. Stick right where you are when any of the Brass comes along. . . . Look, I know you fellows work hard, that you put in long hours when it is necessary. Don't ever run. Stick.'

"With that he slapped the big fellow on the back and walked away. Believe me, that bunch had a lot of respect for Mr. Goodwillie after that."

* * *

One of Rossford's best-loved men was the late Edwin C. Bowers, Sr., who was hired by Capt. Ford himself.

Mr. Bowers was born December 8, 1863, at Hanoverton, a small community near Salem, Ohio. He was one of seven children. His father was a tinsmith.

Ed Bowers was a miller by trade and for years worked for the Pillsburys in Minneapolis. His health demanded outdoor work, so he "Drifted" down the Mississippi, and began working on Ohio river barges and packets between Pittsburgh and Louisville.

He was an expert at checkers, and this ability led to a friendship with a Capt. Slocum, river associate of Capt. Ford in his steamboat days in New Albany. One day while Capt. Slocum and Ed Bowers were playing checkers in the Rivermen's Recreation Hall at Pittsburgh, Capt. Slocum said: "By the way, I have a friend who is building a new glass plant back up the Allegheny at Patterson Station (later christened Ford City). He's looking for good young men."

Bowers was interested and Capt. Slocum took him to Mr. Ford's office in Allegheny (now a part of Pittsburgh). Bowers admired the old gentleman immediately. "He was gruff, but pleasant," Mr. Bowers once recalled.

Capt. Ford introduced young Bowers to Marcus D. Wayman, highly skilled mechanic, then the Old Captain's right hand man. (Wayman had been with Ford in New Albany, where he had married a daughter of one of Capt. Ford's sisters.)

Bowers' first job was at Ford City, before the plant there had been completed. He was assigned to make sketches and photographs, and an inventory of all castings for the glass-making machinery turned out in

Mark Wayman, master mechanic. He followed Capt. Ford from New Albany to Creighton, and then came on to Rossford with Edward Ford.

the company's new machine shop at Ford City. The thousands of pieces of equipment were strewn over the fields where the plant was to be erected.

Bowers became stores keeper; later he was made chief booker. He kept records of all glass produced.

Mr. Bowers met Harriett Elizabeth Clark of Ford City some time later. They were married.

Mark Wayman was Bowers' best man at the wedding. As a matter of record, Wayman was the only man there. Bowers was married at 11:30 a.m. Only a half hour later he was back at his desk in the Ford City plant!

Bowers later became assistant to the then Ford City plant manager, a Mr. Chisholm, and was placed in charge of the lehrs. Cooling glass by lehr methods was a brand new idea then. There were no pyrometers. Temperatures were always judged by looking at the glass. It was no job for the inexperienced.

Mr. Bowers took a lehr job at Kittanning Glass Works in Wick City for a time, then accepted a lucrative offer from Columbia Plate Glass Company in Blairsville, Pennsylvania.

He was offered a job by Edward Ford, and Mr. Bowers served as plant manager at Rossford from December, 1915, until his death in 1934.

During those later years, he often visited with President Edward Ford's eldest son, John B. Ford, head of Wyandotte Chemical at the time, but also a director of his father's Rossford Glass Works.

One of their favorite recollections was the time John B., returning from vacation, found his office occupied only by Mr. Bowers. (The two young men had had desks in the same office.) John B., looking very puzzled, scratched his head and wandered here and there, refusing to ask questions. Someone finally "broke down" and confessed that John B. had been promoted, during his vacation, to Ford City plant manager, and he was escorted to his new office by Mr. Bowers.

* * *

The story of "The Roots Grow Deep" ends logically in 1930, for with the merger of Edward Ford Plate Glass Company with the Libbey-Owens Glass Company in that year, Rossford ceased to be an entity unto itself.

However, 26 years after that merger, a tragedy that stunned thousands of people—the accidental death in 1956 of Edwin C. Bowers, Rossford plant manager, in the prime of his life—makes it appropriate to observe his passing in this book, for *his* roots grew deep, too.

* * *

When she returned home from the cemetery that day after they had buried her husband, the widow of Eddie Bowers saw a great stack of letters.

The stack grew and grew. Most of the letters had been mailed from Rossford homes. Days turned into weeks but Mrs. Bowers read each one, some of them two or three times.

The letters were not the usual missives of condolence . . . they were a torrential downpour of deep affection from men and women who knew him as a boy, as a young man, as a plant manager.

Born in Ford City, Eddie arrived in Rossford when he

Left to right: Jacob Sindyla, John Scharf, Eddie, Frank Liedigk, Joe Mainz and Warren Davis

Some time ago, when Eddie Bowers was asked for his portrait to use in this book, Eddie grinned and said: "No portraits. Use one of those Oldtimers' picnic views." Eddie died soon after that, but here is the kind of picture he meant—surrounded by oldtimers who knew his father and knew Eddie.

Look close and maybe you can recognize some of these old-timers in the early polishing department. That's Matt Pepper and Vince Fildes at extreme left.

was 18. That was in 1915, when his father came at the personal request of Edward Ford to take charge as plant manager.

Eddie had graduated from high school in Blairsville, Pa., took an extra year at Kiski Prep School in Saltsburg, Pa., then graduated from the University of Michigan in 1921.

Born in a community where they knew nothing but glass, growing up among glass men, Eddie was, you might say, born to glass.

His father, however, was very much against Eddie becoming a glass man, particularly at Rossford, where, he felt, his son would be under the handicap of having a father who was boss of the operations.

Eddie decided upon a teaching career, and obtained a position at Fishburne Military School in Waynesboro, Virginia.

One day Bowers received a letter. It was from George Ross Ford, Sr., then president of Edward Ford Plate. He wanted Eddie to come back and work in the plant.

Eddie came back—starting July 1, 1925.

Eddie moved from pot house to batch, casting hall to other departments—absorbing, absorbing and absorbing until glass absorbed his life.

The light burned late in his office quite often, but not always with production problems. Some times it was a

youngster, involved in a fight, or perhaps an older man faced with financial problems. Eddie would probe, sympathize, argue—trying to get at the bottom of things. He saved many a man's job, kept him from walking off or from being fired.

No man was ever seen so often at the Rossford Funeral Home. Eddie was always on hand to console a father or mother, some relative; and he visited the ill in their homes and in hospitals.

There was the time when he returned to Rossford from Kittanning where he had gone to bury his father. Exhausted from the many details, the greeting of those who had come from all over Pennsylvania, Eddie Bowers arrived home late in the afternoon, only to learn that one of his men had just been badly injured.

Dick Cashman, whose father, Sam, had been with Capt. Ford way back in the New Albany days, had been desperately hurt on the job. Eddie put on his coat and drove to St. Vincent's Hospital, arriving at 7 p.m.

He stayed with Mrs. Cashman until 3 a.m. before going home to get the rest he so desperately needed. He was with Mrs. Cashman two weeks later, when they buried her husband.

Winning distinguished honors in amateur tennis for years, Eddie Bowers one day walked into the office of Dr. J. W. Rae, who had just moved to Toledo after practicing in Bowling Green from 1910 to 1932. Eddie wanted treatment for a "tennis elbow" injury. That was the day, in 1934, that he met Frances, Dr. Rae's daughter. They were married within two years.

Twenty-two years later, a moment after they lowered Eddie's body into its grave that rainy afternoon, one of the pallbearers gripped Mrs. Bowers' hand and whispered:

"Frances, he made us work like hell, but he made us love it, too."

* * *

The Steward brothers. Let's take Roy first. Born Robert L. in 1890, on a Morrow County farm 30 miles northeast of Columbus, Ohio, he became a glassman by the pull of a hunter's trigger, as it were.

The late Emory Durivage, then master mechanic at Edward Ford Plate, was hunting on the Steward farm one day in the mid 1900's. One thing led to another, and Emory got William Steward, the father, interested in glass making. William and son visited Rossford. When it came time to go home, Roy didn't want to return. William just couldn't budge his son, so the Steward family moved to Rossford.

Roy and his father began working at Ford Plate in January, 1909. William retired 19 years later, Roy in 1956—after 47 years. He worked in many different departments, but in 1920 began in automotive maintenance, stayed there until his retirement.

Brother Merrill, younger, is still at it. He attended old Walnut street school, graduated from Waite High (Rossford didn't build a high school soon enough for him) and then began in the wareroom. He worked on

the rebuilding of old Plant No. 1 in 1919-20, thence to the emery house in Plant 2 and then to the pipe shop in 1921, where in 1956, he worked under oldtimer Ed Ellerman.

Merrill asks: who remembers the old octagon-shaped bandstand erected for Rossford's German band? It was at Maple and Superior streets. Perspiring ladies served heaping dishes of ice cream under the stand while the German band umpahed with gusto. Merrill won't admit that he ever took a position where the Tuba player could see him eat a pickle or lemon.

* * *

Felix Mainz is carrying on for his pioneering father, Joe. Born in 1910, Felix began at Edward Ford Plate when he was 18 (1928) as a booker, then took time out to attend Bowling Green University.

Back on the job in 1931, Felix became a crane operator, and worked in the packaging department. He was promoted to a foremanship in the optical glass department in 1942 (war work) and later became a general foreman in Thermopane.

* * *

Tom Pierpoint, grandson of Cooper, the original grinder for Capt. Ford at New Albany, cut the first glass for a specific installation for Edward Ford at Rossford.

A few days after it had been finished, Tom stood by the old Post Office, Madison and St. Clair streets, and watched glaziers install it in windows of the old Produce Exchange building, "catty corner" across the street.

Rossford High's first graduation class

The chain gang. When a street car strike of long ago tied up traffic, the chain-drive trucks of Edward Ford Plate Glass Company came to the rescue in transporting Rossford workers to and from Toledo. Can you identify any of these folk?

CHAPTER 11

The Passing Parade

How large a sheet of plate glass could the oldtimers make? Modern glassmen might be surprised.

Jeff Venable, first casting hall foreman at Rossford, held the same job under Edward Ford at Jeffersonville in the 1870's. When a cast was made for exhibiting at the Louisville Industrial Exposition, a Courier-Journal reporter crossed the river to see it, and insisted upon measuring it himself.

The plate measured 230 x 111 inches (19.2 feet by 9.3).

"I could have made one eight inches longer each way," the reporter quoted Mr. Venable.

* * *

Rossford billiard fans went into Toledo to see the boy wonder, Willie Hoppe, March 17, 1905. The youngster trounced Toledo's pride, Frank Auletta. (Hoppe's manager, his father, thought the lad some day might become a champion.)

That same night Mr. and Mrs. George Pope Mac Nichol, Sr. entertained 100 guests. After 7 p.m. supper, guests were arranged at 16 tables for six-handed euchre . . . a group of musicians played Irish airs from behind a bank of palms . . . next day the Blade carried a drawing of the new 16-story Nicholas Building. Construction had just started.

* * *

Dr. Harvey Wiley, chief chemist of the United States, made headlines in the newspapers of March 21, 1905, with his prediction that the time would come when man would be young at 70, explaining that the average span of life in 1905 was 40 . . . Edward Ford was 62 that year, and going strong. His father had died only two years before, aged 92.

* * *

When Eagle Point contained only a few scattered farms and the south boundary of Rossford was the alley north of Bergen street, E. H. Close Realty opened Halstead Heights, confirming rumors that the glass works was to expand—double, maybe triple Rossford's population.

Thousands of Toledoans were attracted by the real estate promotion—a dirigible flying over the area, taking off at the Eagle Point Road end of the proposed Hannum avenue.

Many a Hannum avenue oldtimer recalls those days. Lots sold at $300.

* * *

The tremendous funeral for one of the pioneer residents of the Colony—Mrs. Cecelia Richards. Lived in the same house 68 years. Raised 10 children—James, Alvin, Sam, Dwight and Mrs. Leon Warner of Toledo; Fred, Irving and Mrs. Emma Parker, Rossford; Mrs. David Ladd, Tiffin, and Mrs. Harold Stull, Holland, Ohio. The Richards residence is the only original house left in the Colony.

Skilled in nursing, Mrs. Richards took care of many in Rossford, and you can find in the community dozens of beautiful quilts and fine crocheting she made during her later years. She almost made world history, too, when she had her last child, Mrs. Parker. Emma weighed 17 pounds at birth.

* * *

That big bakery operated at Superior and Elm for so many years by Mr. and Mrs. Homer Tuller, who came from Bowling Green. They had three children—Ross, Charles and Nellie. . . . Ross became postmaster at

Rossford. Consternation when robbers tied him hand and foot, burned his bare feet with matches to make him talk. Home-bound midnight shift Ford employees scared the robbers away.

* * *

Long-remembered formal wedding of Nellie Tuller to Ross DeMuth, also a onetime Rossford postmaster.

* * *

Only a few witnessed the event, but soon all of Rossford was chuckling about one of their favorites—George Ross Ford, when he crawled under his big Stanley Steamer to thaw it out one cold day. Despite the protests of his father's chauffeur, George, looking like a young bear in his ankle-length fur coat, wallowed in the slush and mud under the car, perfect personification of a line in a popular song of the day, "Get Out and Get Under." When he emerged, almost unrecognizable, but triumphant, he faced his father, Edward, too enraged to speak.

"Man," recalls an oldtimer who saw it all, "you should have seen the rest of us get t'hell out of there."

* * *

The late mother of William Baldwin and his sister, Mrs. George Miller, Dixie Terraces, was a cousin of Abraham Lincoln.

* * *

Walter King, who worked for Capt. Ford and later in Rossford, was considered one of the state's best callers at square dances. . . . Otis Warner, Sr., a Ford employee of long ago, once had an offer from a major league baseball club. . . . The excitement attendant to the discovery of oil bubbling up along Grassy Creek. Several wells were drilled, but little oil was found.

* * *

Pre-1920 Rossford news item: "Mr. and Mrs. Robert Enis and daughter Mildred, Mr. and Mrs. Harvey Gampher and Miss Helen, and Mr. and Mrs. Charles Gampher and children, Katherine and Charles Jr., motored up to Sand Lake Sunday. Mr. Gampher tried to stop a truck and left his radiator and hood as souvenirs."

* * *

(Mildred Enis married Warren Burwell, brother of Mel Burwell of Libbey-Owens-Ford. . . . Charles Gampher has passed on. His son, Charles Jr., who made that trip, became a postmaster at Rossford.)

* * *

Oldtimers like to recall that time in the Rossford club house when the late Mike Emmick, short of stature and pugnacious, got into the ring with his boss, Bob Enis, then a machinist in the Ford Works. Bob slipped into another room and poured catsup over his boxing gloves. When Mike rushed out of his corner, Bob let go with a swooshing "haymaker." Startled by what he felt on his face, Mike swiped the back of his glove across his cheek, looked at the "blood" and with a frightened yelp jumped out of the ring.

Sam Frautschi, left, with Mr. and Mrs. Fred Schillinger of Perrysburg road, Rossford, at the latter's winter home in Winterhaven, Fla. (Mr. Schillinger is said to be the contractor who poured cement for the Cherry street bridge.)

* * *

One of the most beloved of all Rossford citizens was the late Samuel Frautschi, a clerk in the old Summit street Neuhausel store before opening his combined dry goods and grocery in Rossford. Sons Fred, Arnold and Walter catered to the grocery trade, while father Sam, who was never known to have a frown on his face, waited upon those wanting silks and calicoes, shoes and shirts.

Grownups today remember Mr. Frautschi's inability to turn away youngsters . . . empty thread boxes made cunning doll cradles . . . and he was always slipping a penny doll to some little girl . . . samples of cloth made dresses or comforters for the dollies.

* * *

Contrast today's roaring traffic on wide, well-paved Miami street with old dirt road from Rossford to Toledo, so narrow that hazel brush scratched the buggies. . . . They began to widen and stone the road in 1906.

* * *

Rossford's first theater: The Pearl. A player piano thumped out exciting numbers as Pearl White was about to jump off a cliff, or the Iron Claw reached for somebody. Theater was owned by Charles Phillipe.

* * *

Marion Carlson married William Rubley, who worked in the Edward Ford wareroom, and later as a cutter in the laminating plant on East Broadway before retiring. Mrs. Rubley has been with the company 32 years, the last 29 of them as chief telephone operator at the Rossford plant. Her father, Tom Carlson, began with Edward Ford as a cutter and retired in 1906.

* * *

Rossford crowded with visitors for the Fourth of July. Big dinner baskets loaded with fried chicken, pickled eggs, potato salad, immense pies and cakes, sugar cookies, sweet pickles and great pots of baked beans . . . the platform atop Uhlman's Dry Goods store to shoot off the community fireworks . . . two big poles, the tallest for Old Glory, the smaller one greased for dozens of small boys to try climbing it for a prize . . . the berry pie contest in which contestants got stained from forehead to knees . . . the big dance floor in the street where fiddlers squeaked out "Devil's Dream" and "Irish Washer Woman."

FIRST OLDTIMERS' PICNIC resulted from a request to obtain a photograph of veteran employees. This posed a problem, since many worked on day shifts and others at night.

However, the men agreed to get together for the picture. They had such fun in greeting each other again that the idea of "doing this oftener" was discussed. The following Sunday, the first formal picnic was held, with D. H. Goodwillie, Curtis W. Davis (then Rossford plant manager) and George R. Ford, Jr., chipping in to pay for the refreshments.

So, the Oldtimers' Picnic has become an annual affair, with a certain definite pattern— tables under the big trees in Crane's Woods, for euchre, poker and other favorite games; long tables heaped with refreshments; horseshoe contests, and a rigid rule: "No women, no dogs, no kids and no ties."

Here are the 54 men in this picture of the Oldtimers gathered for the first picnic.

Back row, left to right: Charles Badik, Steve Kovatch, Steve Kotowski, Martin Kustra, Pete Kavich, Mike Weiner, John Stackowicz, J. Baker, John Kralik, John Klepacz, Thomas Hatas, Sr., Paul Liedigk, Felix Mazur, Joseph Liedigk, Mose Wright, John Knurek, Tom Wood, Walter Walker, Robert Hufford, George Becker and William King.

Middle row, left to right: Stanley Waclawski, J. Lorence, John Yeo, R. Fosnaught, Leopold Wojton, L. Tutak, Pete Rossler, Adam Jerry, John Baillett, August Liedigk, Alex Szorady, Mike Szczeparski, Pete Ignaczak, Sebastian Visi, Harry Craver, Frank Liedigk, George Knerr, L. Tremsky, Sr., and Mike Cieply.

Front row, left to right: August LaHote, Elmer Conners, William Rossler, Harry Thornton, E. Sullivan, Joseph Mainz, James King, Tom Peltz, Leo Winkler, Irving Richards, Warren Davis, John Radocy, Joe Rossler and William Langendonk.

Steve Yandow, left, teaching some secret horseshoe throwing tricks to veteran Harvey P. Gampher. This is at one of the Rossford Old-timers' picnics. Steve began as a blacksmith with Edward Ford Plate Glass in 1910.

Another pre-1920 Rossford news item: "George Skaggs of Rossford, our scrappy soldier-fighter, will go up against Louis Klewer; Klewer, a Marine, is American featherweight champion." (Lou Klewer later became a Toledo sports writer, today travels to the far places to get material for his "Outdoors" column.)

* * *

Another old social item: "Miss Mildred Enis (Mrs. Warren Burwell) thinks 13 is a lucky number, as it was that number of years of age she had attained last Saturday when a number of her young friends visited her home on Jennings road. The following sub-debs and their attaches attended:

"The Misses Alma Winters, Marian Duncan, Helen Renaud, Alice Rinker, Winifred Sawyer, Viola Michael, Ida Schiffgen and Mabel Westfall; Max Woods, Walter Heinemann, Philip, Lester and Milo Philbin, Frank Krakau, Jr., Charles Gampher, Jr., Frank LaVrar and Homer Steward."

* * *

There's something fascinating about a nickname. Here are some from the long ago!

Tot, Toots and Red Springer . . . Fuzzy Huett . . . Tootsie (Frank) Krakau . . . Squirrel Heinemann . . . Lobster and Prunes Heinrich . . . Buster and Crab Brown . . . Pid (Walter) King . . . Zizzy (Dwight) Richards . . . Bull Sarver, twin of Chester . . . Boshie (Sebastian) Rinker . . . Porky Shabinaw . . . Hansie (Dorothy) Krakau . . . Irving Brown's daughter, Mary Alice, was called Jim . . . (She's now the wife of a famous surgeon.) Catfish (Thomas) McCreery . . . Frog (Clarence) Monoit . . . Rusty (Agnes) Schiffgen . . . Ute (Ruth) Krakau . . .

* * *

The old Toledo, Maumee, Perrysburg and Rossford "belt line" played an important part in building up Rossford.

The line was incorporated December 26, 1893, with an announced capital stock of $300,000. The promoter was J. K. Tilletson, who two years before had opened Hotel Victory at Put-In-Bay and the Victory Park railway there. He announced 30-minute service between Toledo and Perrysburg would be available. Four open and two closed cars were purchased, the open jobs at $1,780 each and the closed cars costing $2,665 each. Each car accommodated 96 passengers, with reversible seats. The cars were painted royal blue and were purchased from the St. Louis Car Company.

On July 6, 1894, it was announced by the press that Mr. Tilletson had been replaced by Parks Foster of Elyria. A contract with Consolidated Edison Company of Toledo called for service between Toledo and Maumee by August 1 that year, and to Perrysburg by July 1, 1897.

A new Maumee-Perrysburg bridge was opened May 10, 1895, and, meantime, the Oak street car line from Toledo to Rossford's town limits on the north having been extended, the "belt line" service was inaugurated.

A ride around the belt became the thing to do. That last car from Toledo on Saturday night was a madhouse, crammed with tired folks who had spent the day at the Casino out Summit street, or at The Farm out Cherry street, or Bellevue Park.

Up along the Perrysburg road was Cook's switch, just around the bend beyond Bates road. By putting an ear to the telephone pole you could hear the car coming long before it came sweeping around the bend.

* * *

Rossford children began attending music and dancing classes in Toledo as a result of the belt line; little boys could hardly wait until they grew up to be motormen on the line. Many a youngster coming from school in Toledo used to skip into the little rest room at the end of the car, waiting until fares had been collected, but he seldom escaped the eagle-eyed conductor . . . and all this for five cents.

* * *

Rossford's first carnival: It was held in a field where later that row of houses now known as the Dixie Terraces and the first Rossford Bank were built years later. Sponsored by Rossford business men, it sent every child in Rossford scrambling to the Glass Works on pay day. Jerking Dad's coat or pulling at his pants leg, they bubbled: "Pa, there's a real merry-go-round over on the ball field."

* * *

Wonder how many of the 57 boys are still around who took part in Rossford's first Easter egg jamboree. Encouraged by Edward Ford, Mary Spencer Hohl began teaching a Sunday School class with a special goal in mind—making a flower garden in the field where the carnival had been. It turned into a beauty spot.

Then an Easter egg party was decided upon—to raise some money for something—it didn't matter what. The 57 boys visited every farmer within five miles of Rossford. Each farmer promised them eggs, free. Henry Lammers, Alfred Harris, the Frautschis and others offered to let the boys drive their delivery wagons into the country to gather up the promised eggs.

A week before Easter, Mrs. Hohl's backyard contained stacks of boxes filled with eggs . . . money poured in. The boys voted to buy a new pulpit suite for the Methodist Church. Chris Finkbeiner, who had a furniture store at Fourth and Main in East Toledo, offered to supply it at whatever total the boys collected. Amount collected for the eggs was $77.

* * *

When workmen were tearing up Rossford's first board walk along Superior street, an army of small boys followed eagerly, armed with sticks. As a section was removed they would dive in, hunting pennies and nickels. . . . One of them, Wilbur Walgemuth, rushed into

Tuller's store, bug-eyed and panting, his muddy little fist grasping what he thought was a 50-cent piece. He bought candy from Ross DeMuth. The latter recognized the value of the coin, but gave young Wilbur 50 cents worth of candy. Wilbur started out. When he reached the door, DeMuth called: "Wait—don't you want your change?"

Wilbur almost dropped his sack of candy as he saw $19.50 in change. He had found a twenty-dollar gold piece. (Edward Ford Plate often paid its men in gold pieces in those days.) Wilbur and some of his chums promptly bought the entire supply of canned goods at the tiny store of an old Civil War Veteran at Superior and Elm, and had a picnic in the big pine woods that was cut down years later to make room for Larro Milling and the old sugar plant, where Thermopane now is made . . . that picnic was held nearly 50 years ago.

* * *

George Ford, Sr. had the first automobile in Rossford—a little bright red roadster. The late Dr. Elmer B. Holst, whose office was across the street from the plant, had the second one—a gray Maxwell.

* * *

Dr. Holst, who opened an office in Rossford about 1900, came from Haskins. He had Rossford's first "residential" phone. His wife often called in coal orders for neighbors to Munch's yard, then at Main and Second, East Toledo.

* * *

John Davis was night caretaker of the Ford office for many years. He and his wife took care of the kitchen and restaurant on the second floor.

* * *

Charley Tuller, Rossford druggist of long ago, a fine dresser, defied tradition and made all Rossford stare by wearing his famous imported Panama Perfecto straw hat on Christmas Day . . . and it was Tuller who startled the community by laying in a supply of ice cream and serving it in WINTER.

Many fondly remember this couple, Mr. and Mrs. John Davis, caretakers. "Aunt Viney" as the Ford children called Mrs. Davis, baked Boston brown bread which was so-o-o good that—well, ask George P. MacNichol and his sister, Laura. As children, they almost foundered on it.

that representatives of 17 different nationalities were working there.

* * *

Perhaps this will serve to end the many friendly arguments among oldtimers as to when the Rossford Club House got started.

It was incorporated under state law on November 30, 1917, soon after the club building was completed. First officers (1918) were as follows:

John J. Scharf . . . . President
George R. Ford . . . . Vice President
C. E. (Cy) Taylor . . . . Treasurer
Vincent P. P. Fildes . . . . Secretary
Executive committee: Edward and George Ford, Clark E. Husted.

* * *

The late Joe Daily was Athletic Director for several years. Verne Evans, who later became a member of Libbey-Owens-Ford's purchasing department, and now retired, was referee for most of the boxing matches, and he was active in all other Ford employee athletic activities, including the famed Ford midgets basketball team.

* * *

January 1, 1903: Rossford has 100 homes, 600 men working in plant. Works operated night and day. Paid out in semi-monthly wages: $16,000 to $17,000. All machinery operated by electricity.

* * *

When Chief Engineer Dave Goodwillie first joined Edward Ford Plate in 1920, he drove a Ford, gift of city employees who had worked under him. Later he

An oldtimer recalls that about 1910, the variety of Christmas cookies and cakes baked by Rossford housewives had reached an amazing total and beautiful variety. . . . That might have been due to the fact that a check of Ford plant payrolls of that year reveals

traded it for a Maxwell; still later he drove a Hup-mobile roadster.

He used to pick up Orel Frary, still in the fold, as she waited for the Oak street car at Miami street and Oregon road. Miss Frary took dictation from George Ford, Mr. Goodwillie and Clark Husted. Miss Frary, who handled customer orders much of the time, still remembers the card number of a famous customer: Card No. 188—Fisher Body.

* * *

Sales managers of Edward Ford Plate, in order of service: George P. MacNichol, Sr.; George W. DeMaid, who came from James H. Rice Company, Chicago, from 1903 to about 1910, when he died; Claude Lewis, book-keeper and later superintendent, appointed sales agent; he left in 1914, replaced by Harry Eckenrode who had been assistant to Lewis for about two years. Eckenrode accepted presidency of National Plate Glass Company in 1917; J. Roy Helm, secretary of National Flat Glass Jobbers Association, Chicago, succeeded him. He was replaced about 1926 by George P. MacNichol, Jr.

* * *

Rossford's first football game was never finished. It began late in the afternoon of September 6, 1901, in a field now occupied by the old Rossford bank and houses (The Dixie Terraces).

Twenty-two Rossford huskies, wearing turtle neck sweaters, were playing a game new to the community. The coach and star of the two teams was a tall, wavy-haired young man with an English accent. He was London-born Tom Wood (father of Max).

He played on first one team and then the other to instill the fine points of the game into his fellow factory workers. Foreign-born citizens came a-running, sensing a big free-for-all fight. They stared in astonishment, however, at the strange antics of the group, kneeling down, then charging and clawing at each other like enraged animals, then kneeling down in straight lines once more, only to leap and lunge again. Sweaters began to rip, blood-smeared faces polka dotted the scene.

A street car from Toledo brought Dr. Elmer Holst to the scene, his face flushed with excitement. The group huddled around him, and then 100 or so onlookers watched in astonishment as the players suddenly broke and ran in all directions, shouting and yelling.

Dr. Holst had just told them the news—President McKinley had been shot.

* * *

Only baseball rivaled football in Rossford sports. . . . Some of the early players were the Brown boys—Herb, Emory, Ernie (Buster), Walter and Art, who graduated to the Southern Association; the King boys—Jim, Charley, Merce and Walter, headed by their uncles, Bill and John, both of whom made tidy livings for years in the minor leagues.

Two of the most popular players were Bruno (Prunes) Heidrich and Charlie King, both pitchers. Prunes was a left hander, who many say could have gone to the major leagues, had he been interested. Charlie King's ability to hit placed him at first base or in the outfield when he wasn't pitching. He later played with Milwaukee in the American Association.

A very early Rossford baseball team. Can you recognize any of them?

This batch of basketball beauties are now mothers, and some of them grandmothers.
First row, left to right: Adell Schiffgen, Mildred Enis, Gladys Fitzgerald, Helen Renaud.
Back row, from left: Madelina McLaughlin, Alice Geltz, Cecelia Vrablic, Ida Schiffgen, Julia Hetman; Verda Sampsel, coach.

Louise Sutton Wagner

Few are richer in memories than Louise Sutton Wagner. Joining the company in 1909, she served as secretary to Edward Ford, took Clark Husted's dictation and worked in billing under Sales Manager DeMaid. She recalled when George Ford Sr. had a little experimental workshop hidden away out in the plant where he tinkered with automobile engines, and invented one of his own—which never reached the market.

Miss Sutton remembered that George Ford and Clark Husted were classmates at old Tri-State University in Toledo. Years later, Louise Sutton figured every inch of glass that went into the famed Empire State Building.

When 200 rough diamonds arrived from Belgium for cutting glass at Rossford, the German letter accompanying the shipment was translated for President Edward Ford by Miss Sutton.

"One thing I shall never, never forget," Louise said, a faraway look in her eyes, "it was the *way* I learned of Edward Ford's death. Laura MacNichol called me by telephone at my home.

" 'Louise, your pal just died.' "

* * *

"On the Sunny Side of the Street"

Moses Wright is something of a legendary figure in Rossford. Born in Alabama in 1883, Moses drifted north to seek work. He found it in a plate glass factory near Crystal City, Missouri.

In 1916, Moses followed a trainload of families eastward to Rossford.

Moses worked hard, always cheerful, humming and singing, mostly to himself. Edward Ford came to know him, liked him, often talking with him as Moses, naked to the waist, toiled in the swirling heat from the pots of molten glass, sweat turning his body into polished ebony.

When Moses and a few of his brethern wanted to build a church, Edward Ford offered funds—repayable only when the tiny congregation could afford it.

They built on Osborne street in 1918. And in 1922, Moses took Una Lee Brown as his bride—first wedding in the church. Moses was really walking on the Sunny Side of the Street now, as some of the men put it.

Moses and Una Lee had ten children. Four of the daughters were married in the little church. One son became a minister.

Moses hummed and sang, his hair greying, his shoulders stooping a bit more. One day in 1944, he took some time off to watch his son, Ned, graduate from Rossford High School. Ned was a singer, a good one. His teacher, Franklin Nold of Perrysburg, encouraged the lad.

Ned served a hitch in the army, returned to work at the glass plant, then to the conservatory of music at Oberlin College. Returning home, he received his GI money, used it to enter the famed Juilliard School of Music in New York City.

If only Moses could have waited, but in 1950, his earthly walks on the Sunny Side of the Street came to an end . . . in January, 1956, Life magazine carried a

RHS boys basketball club, 1923-4, same year as the girls' at left.
Front row, left to right: Silas Wolfe, John King, Norman Ringle, Milo Philbin.
Back row, from left: Chet Mavolf, Art Howard, H. S. Burtch and G. Knollmiller.

Walter Durielet, Merrill Steward, Ernie Lewis,
Arthur Kneer and James Bowers

picture of Ned, member of the cast of Porgy and Bess touring Russia. The picture showed Ned singing to the enraptured Russians.

Ned's song? . . . "On the Sunny Side of the Street."

* * *

Van Hudepohl, an office worker for the Fords from the Creighton days, was a "bug" on statistics. His annual production figures, showing a total of 231,362,699 square feet of plate glass produced from October, 1898, to June 30, 1930, were interestingly "translated" in one of his note books as follows:

"If cut into square foot pieces and laid end to end, this glass would extend 43,818½ miles or 14½ times the distance across the United States; or if placed atop each other the pieces would make a pile 913 miles high; would require for transportation 15,424 cars of 50,000-feet capacity, a train 99⅕ miles long."

* * *

James B. Cryan. Jim probably has been the butt of more practical jokes than any man in Rossford. George Ford and Dave Goodwillie "accidently" ran right over Jim's brand new black derby . . . George Ford, Jr. painted Jim's new Essex. Hunting for it, Jim didn't recognize the glowing purple car as his. The glow stuff washed off.

Like his father before him, Jim was a railroad man. When he arrived upon the Rossford scene in December, 1916, he received a mighty cold job—checking freight cars in the yard. His duties broadened—rate checking, expediting in and out-bound shipments, filing claims. Then he became supervisor of stores.

He worked with them all—from Edward Ford on through the roster. They called Edward Ford "The Governor," Jim recalls. Why? He doesn't know, but they didn't call him that to his face. It was a term of affection, however, brought in by some of the men from the Pennsylvania days.

* * *

Fred Prentice, first white child born in Toledo (then Port Lawrence) was a pre-Rossford pioneer. He walked with the Indians.

Fred's father, Joseph, sold his land holdings in Port Lawrence and bought large acreage in what became Rossford, built a log cabin in the deep woods and moved his family across the Maumee to it in 1825—(the year John B. Ford ran away from home).

When he was 23, Fred, the son, having saved money from the sale of wood to steamboats plying the Maumee, built a great house on property now occupied by the Glass Works. Later he moved to New York state.

Mr. Prentice died at his estate, Cornwall-on-the-Hudson, in 1913, aged 91.

* * *

Financial mother and granite bulwark for thousands of Rossfordians. That would be the Rossford Savings Bank, founded by Edward Ford.

It opened for business July 1, 1918. Account No. 1, still active, was taken out by 10-year-old George Ross Ford, Jr., on opening day.

Close behind was Mrs. George Smithers, wife of a Rossford area farmer. Account No. 15 was opened by George Saelzer, veteran Ford glass worker. (By 1956, there were nearly 9,000 depositors.)

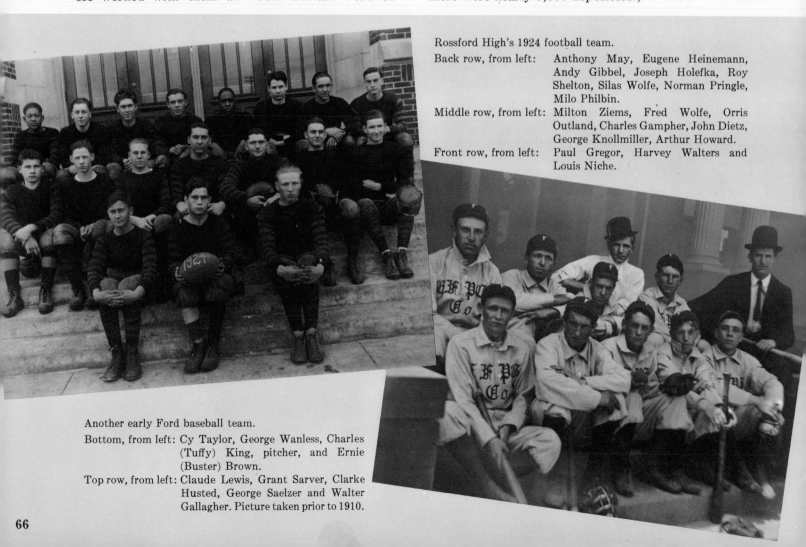

Rossford High's 1924 football team.
Back row, from left: Anthony May, Eugene Heinemann, Andy Gibbel, Joseph Holefka, Roy Shelton, Silas Wolfe, Norman Pringle, Milo Philbin.
Middle row, from left: Milton Ziems, Fred Wolfe, Orris Outland, Charles Gampher, John Dietz, George Knollmiller, Arthur Howard.
Front row, from left: Paul Gregor, Harvey Walters and Louis Niche.

Another early Ford baseball team.
Bottom, from left: Cy Taylor, George Wanless, Charles (Tuffy) King, pitcher, and Ernie (Buster) Brown.
Top row, from left: Claude Lewis, Grant Sarver, Clarke Husted, George Saelzer and Walter Gallagher. Picture taken prior to 1910.

There have been only three presidents of the bank. George Ross Ford succeeded his father upon the latter's death in 1920; George Ross Ford, Jr., became president after the death of his father in 1938.

Earl B. Hass was first cashier. One July day in 1920, while playing in a noon baseball game with some of the glassworkers at a nearby "diamond," Mr. Hass collapsed, died before anybody could reach him.

A hurry-up call was sent to the old First National Bank in Toledo. "Send over a man who can serve as cashier for just a few days, until we can get squared away," George Ross Ford telephoned.

Henry Werner was sent over for a few days. As this is being written, the few days have multiplied into 37 years!

* * *

Edward Ford built Rossford's first school, a four-room building known as the Walnut Street School.

Laura C. Venable, daughter of Jeff Venable, first casting hall foreman, taught all grades. She was 20.

By 1901, the Misses Ethel Stocking and Delia Atkinson were added to the staff, with Jasper Shriver as principal.

Morrison R. Van Cleve replaced Shriver, went on to higher educational grounds; Vernon Riggle was third principal, later became Ohio State Superintendent of Schools.

C. P. Hanselman came in from Leipsic, during expansion of the school. Serving as superintendent, 1913 to 1918, he resigned to accept Cy Taylor's offer to join the expanding timekeeper's office at the Glass Works,

working with Jake Bayer and Gus Boenke, later under Bill Fague, who replaced Cy Taylor in 1923.

Mr. Hanselman liked to recall two instances:

"I helped Junior MacNichol with the books when he came in from college as assistant treasurer. One day I addressed him as *Mr.* MacNichol. By the look on his face," Mr. Hanselman chuckled, "I thought he was going to slap me . . . no finer man ever wore shoes than that lad.

"I got pretty well acquainted with his grandfather, Edward Ford, even before I joined the company. It was while I was principal at Walnut School. We had just had the school enlarged (by Mr. Ford's own money, I suspect) but we still needed some equipment. I made up a list and presented it to Mr. Ford. It was quit long. Mr. Ford went over it carefully. Then he just looked at me. I bowed out, very quietly. Maybe I had been a mite too ambitious . . . a few days later a huge truck drove up to the school and unloaded complete equipment for manual training, domestic science and a gymnasium—all new.

"No bill was presented. None ever was. I don't believe anybody ever knew who supplied all that wonderful equipment."

* * *

Clean up: Mr. Hanselman, recalling that Edward Ford donated $1,000 so that Rossford could have District Nurse services, says the first nurse was a Miss Kilmer.

"Some of those youngsters came to school with quite a bit of soil on them," C. P. recalls. "I used to wash up the boys while Nurse Kilmer took care of the little girls.

"Mr. Ford, in sending over all that equipment, included some bathtubs. Nurse Kilmer and I had a field day. Then I received a note from a mother whose youngster I had bathed, bought him a new shirt and sent him home with the soiled one under his arm.

"The mother's note said: 'Any time my boy needs a bath, *I'll* give to him.' "

* * *

E. N. Littleton followed Hanselman as principal. The others who followed: F. R. McLaughlin, J. W. Welsh, H. R. Troutner, Harold Kohler and Leona Schaaf.

* * *

Children of Catholic parents in Rossford attended Good Shepherd School in East Toledo until 1903, when ground purchased from William Tracy in 1902 was utilized. The old Tracy barn was remodeled into a combination church and school. They named it St. Mary Magdalene. Franciscan Sisters of Sylvania instructed.

The first marriage was that of Anna Kostur and Frank Poldyak, with Father Leo Redmer officiating. That was on October 10, 1903. Earlier in the year, Marie Van Ryn, daughter of Peter and Wilhelmina Van Ryn, was the first child to be baptized. Her sponsors were John Schiffgen and Anna Kopp.

A new church and school were built in 1925.

Rossford Junior High basketball team, 1919.
Back row, from left: Bill Fitzgerald, Frank LaVrar, Mr. Littleton, Homer Steward and Ray King.
Front row, from left: Earl Lewis, Bud Carson and Walter Heinemann.

Third and Fourth Graders. Scratch your head over these cute rascals.

Floyd R. McLaughlin was the first superintendent of schools in Rossford, there being nine grades, all housed in the Walnut Street School.

Following his graduation from Jerry City High School, he began teaching when he was 16, at $35 per month. He was later at Cygnet and Rudolph, thence to Rossford.

When he retired many years later, Mr. McLaughlin had presided over the graduation of 932 young men and women of Rossford. He was an early campaigner for the bond drive to build Rossford High, the Eagle Point School, the Walnut School expansion and the drive to obtain funds for Rossford High's stadium and field house. He was superintendent of Rossford schools for 27 years.

* * *

Rossford High was built in 1923, ending the era of Rossford youngsters having to attend high school classes in Toledo. The first principal was Paul H. Weaver. First graduating class (1924) included Mildred Enis, Alice Geltz, Chester Marlof, Lester Philbin and Ida Schiffgen.

Principals succeeding Mr. Weaver were Howard S. Burtch, Carl F. Doebler, G. H. Burns (who later replaced McLaughlin as superintendent of schools); Fred O. Ellsworth and Edgar E. Andrews.

Rossford High's first orchestra: Helen Renaud, cornet; Mary Mainz, piano; Katherine Mainz and Frank Krakau, Jr., violins; Lester Philbin, cornet. Teacher: Miss Bertha Beneen.

* * *

Eagle Point Public School began in 1929 with 12 rooms on Eagle Point road property purchased from Bob Enis. Principals: Harley Carnicome, Melvin Osborne, Richard Douard, Robert L. Frank and Eugene R. Sheline.

CLASS OF OLD
WALNUT STREET SCHOOL

Front row, left to right: Emma Rinker, Dollie Ferdig, Nellie Metzler, Lloyd Walters, Eugene Kimmell, Wood Cauffield, Elizabeth Smith, Ella Uffman and Flora Kier.

Middle row, from left: Nellie Russell, Helen Swinderman, Francis Whitlock, Bessie Cook, Hattie Whitlock, Clara Frautschi, Ethel Henderson and Emma Williams.

Back row, from left: Eva Ballard, Martha Heidrich, Zella Cauffield, Mr. Shriver, teacher; Mattie Smithers, Jessie Sullivan and Nellie Smith.

ROSSFORD PUBLIC SCHOOL.

First graduating class (1947) of Sts. Cyril and Methodius School: Audrey Bonzani, Helen Cepko, Mildred Mihalek, Elizabeth Olic, Martha Palka, Patricia Peer, Helen Stepan, Thomas and Anthony Badik, Anthony Durco, Emil Hricovsky, Robert Marcinek and William Screptock.

First Sunday School class conducted in Rossford was by Dr. J. M. Avvan, presiding elder of the Toledo district of the Methodist Episcopal Church, in the little Walnut Street School on October 29, 1899. First church services were held by Dr. Avvan in the same place the following November 5.

Hearing of the parish's desire for a church, Capt. John B. Ford donated $1,000. With that money the

Mrs. J. L. Henry, president, Mrs. Lydia King, vice president, and Mrs. Linweber, were the first officers of the M. E. Ladies Aid Society, formed March 13, 1902.

First wedding in the Methodist Church built in 1922 was that of Helen Gampher, daughter of Harvey, to Jeff Springer.

By 1912 there were 15 Ukrainian Catholic families in Rossford. They organized St. Michael's Church in 1912. First marriage was between Pelazia Bober and John Cholewka, with the Rev. Father Paul Stawrowsky officiating. That was November 10, 1912. Mary Krzij was the first child to be baptized, February 16, 1913.

A larger church was built in 1948. First child to be baptized in the new church was Paul Michael Kornowa, June 5, 1949. First marriage was between Mary Denko

Class of 1915. Sixth graders

small Disciples Church on Maple street was purchased in 1902.

Following Capt. Ford's death on May 1 of the following year, memorial services were held in the little church. Its mortgage was paid off 17 days later by Edward Ford. He gave the church generous financial aid for many years after that.

Original members: Mrs. Priscilla Cooper, Mrs. Phoebe Gray, the Misses Edna and Laura Johnson, Mr. and Mrs. Charles Kier, Mrs. Elida King, Mr. and Mrs. E. Martin, Frank Martin, Miss Priscilla Pepper, Mrs. Matthias Pepper, Sr., Thomas Pierpont, Mr. and Mrs. William Simms, Mr. and Mrs. George Smithers, Laura Venable, Mr. and Mrs. E. M. Warner, Mrs. Adele Westfall, Miss Ida Zerney, Mrs. Louise Zerney.

Sunday School teachers in 1899 and 1900: E. M. Warner, Ethel Stocking, Mrs. J. R. Colgan, Luella Colgan, Priscilla Pepper and Laura and Mame Venable. Jennie Warner (Mrs. H. M. Linweber) was chorister.

and Peter Heban, July 2, 1949, the Rev. Father Walter Rozko officiating as first pastor of the larger church.

First Slovak people came to Rossford about 1903. Plans for a parish were formulated in 1915. About 60 families convened in St. Michael's Ukrainian Church to listen to organization suggestions by the Most Rev. Joseph Schrembs, then bishop of Toledo.

The vacated Methodist Church on Maple street was purchased in 1922, remodeled and opened August 26, 1923, when the Most Rev. Samuel A. Stritch, who succeeded Bishop Schrembs, presided at dedicatory ceremonies. The Slovak dedication sermon was preached by the Rev. Alexander Sindelar, then touring America in behalf of the Literary Society of St. Adalbert of Slovakia.

First pastor was Father Anthony A. Pirnat. Ethel, daughter of Mr. and Mrs. Andrew Minarcin, was the first to receive baptism, August 26, 1923. Two days later, the first marriage was between Michael Stolar and Caroline Sarancik.

The top view of the black derby—it shelters Edward Ford. Fresh in from a Florida vacation, he is helping to set up a new kind of lawn game (about 1902) to demonstrate to the office force how to play the game. He brought it back especially for them to get a little exercise and fun during luncheon periods.

Residence and property of John Baillet were purchased in 1945; the old church was dismantled the following year, replaced by a new residence for the pastor; a new church was completed in 1947.

* * *

Dr. Charles M. Harpster was Rossford's first physician. He built on Superior street, installing a drug store on the first floor, with his office and operating room at the back, his residence on the second floor.

After serving as surgeon for Edward Ford Plate and physician to the community, Dr. Harpster decided to study in Germany. He sold his property in 1901 to Dr. Elmer B. Holst.

Dr. Holst, born in Toledo, attended Toledo schools until he was 10, then moved with his parents to a farm, 20 acres on the Eagle Point side of Grassy Creek and 12 acres on the Perrysburg side.

He first practiced in Haskins, then went to Rossford as surgeon to Edward Ford Plate, the community and to the old C. H. & D. Railroad. He died in 1913, aged 38. His old home later became the Rossford mortuary.

Dr. L. J. Herold, born in Toledo, replaced Dr. Holst. He played in Rossford's band and was very active in community affairs until 1928, when he left for further study. He opened an office in Toledo in 1929.

Dr. Clarence L. Ordway, well known in Bowling Green, practiced in East Toledo for many years, and had a residence and office in Rossford for a long time.

Dr. J. C. Gallagher, a Nebraskan, practiced among plate glass workers of Valley Park, Missouri, 1904 until 1916, when he accompanied many fire and flood victim families to Rossford. He retired in 1938.

His son, Dr. John E. Gallagher, moved into his father's offices. Dr. Gerald G. Wood began practicing in Rossford in 1934, resides at 425 Riverside Drive.

Dr. Walter A. Johnson, born in Toledo, early became associated with Dr. Gallagher. He served in World War II with the 82nd Air Borne Glider Division as a captain. He has his own office in Rossford now. He is the son of Mr. and Mrs. Otto Johnson of East River road. Otto once was coachman and later chauffeur for Edward Ford.

Dr. John L. Eickholt was Rossford's first dentist, opening an office at Oak and Superior streets in 1919.

Dr. Henry B. Green opened a dental office in Rossford in 1934, practicing evenings. He moved from Toledo and opened an office at 413 Superior street in 1938 on a full-time basis.

Dr. C. F. Berry, who served as a dental surgeon in World War I, opened an office at 223 Superior street in 1945.

* * *

Rossford's Mayors

Frederick Uffman, Jr., born on his father's farm in what is now Eagle Point Colony, served seven terms as Rossford's mayor. He volunteered to serve his first two-year term without salary, due to the low financial state of the newly incorporated town—incorporated in its 40th year as a community.

Mayor Uffman accomplished many things, including Rossford's first free mail service, for which he had worked untiringly. He resigned after his fifth consecutive term.

Mr. Uffman's father first had a vegetable farm, later established a greenhouse, now operated by Fred, Jr. and his brother, William.

After two terms out of office, Mayor Uffman was re-elected twice for a total of seven terms . . . Mr. Uffman married Grace M. Karg, whose father, Charles, operated a shoe store on Main street, East Toledo, for many years. Mr. and Mrs. Uffman reside at 46 Riverside Drive, Rossford.

Charles L. Appt, glass worker at Rossford and son of Charles and Rose Appt, became mayor after Mr. Uffman's resignation following his fifth term.

This old hotel, first commercial building completed in the new village, 1898-99, still serves on its original site on Oak street, near Superior.

Mr. Appt, who served two terms and accomplished many improvements during his administration, married a daughter of Howard Warner, son of Rossford pioneer Elliott Warner.

Following first-mayor Uffman's final term, Hugh Zuckowski, another glass worker, was elected mayor.

* * *

Clubs and Posts

The Slovak Gymnastic Union was organized in 1914 by Rudolph Sitlava, Sr., Andrew Minarcin and Steve Holkovic. Originally, there were 15 members, with the following officers: Minarcin, president; Holkovic, treasurer; and Martin Varblic, secretary.

The Union erected a building at 124 Bacon street in 1928. There are more than 350 members now.

The Ukrainian American Citizens Club was established in 1926, organized by the Rev. George Krupa, Lawrence Holefka, Michael Kopystynsky, Nicholas Proch, Johann Fedaruk and Nicholas Bobak.

The Polski Dom Handlowy Corp. (Polish Commercial House) was organized in 1921. A building was erected on Bergen street. Organizers included: Joseph Suchowiki, president and builder; Joseph Poldyak, vice president; Adam Gorka, financial secretary; Marian Pietrass, recording secretary; Casimir Knurek, treasurer.

First officers of Rossford F.O.E. were: L. J. Baker, president; Tom Kurth, vice president; Donald Kemp, secretary. First enrolled member was Henry (Whitey) Beuth. When chartered, it had the largest Eagle membership in Ohio, 'tis said . . . 100 members.

First meetings were held in the Ford Club House, later in Sokol Hall, still later in the lodge's own new building on Dixie Highway.

In the old days of public water faucets. That's Clarence LeRoy filling his bucket.

Rossford Post, American Legion, was organized in 1922, with Henry Werner, Jr. as commander. Other first officers: Guy Hill, vice commander; Donald Sage, adjutant; William Maddock, librarian; O. C. Reynolds, chaplain; Herbert Brown, finance officer; Louis Stoncek, sergeant - at - arms; E. C. Bowers, Jr., publicity.

An auxiliary was formed, with these first officers; Helen Wallace, president; Lillian Baldwin, vice president; Laura Zobler, treasurer; Leona Gallagher, sergeant-at-arms; Anna Cairns, publicity; Mabel Brown, secretary; Mabel Haworth, chaplain.

First V.F.W. unit, the William (Bucky) Klepacz Post, was organized with Joseph F. Ziemianski as first commander.

One of the largest and most active women's organization is the Rossford Women's Club, founded in 1933. An organizational meeting was held in the residence of Mrs. William Maddock in November of that year.

Charter members were: Mrs. Amos L. Conn, credited with having first suggested the club; Mrs. G. Richard Cashman, Mrs. Joseph C. Gallagher, Mrs. C. P. Hanselman, Mrs. Edward P. Harker, Mrs. Roy Kelly, Mrs. Walter E. Kruger, Mrs. Floyd R. McLaughlin, Mrs. Charles H. Potter, Mrs. Clarence N. Sawyer, Mrs. Roscoe C. Schaeffer, Mrs. John Schaffer, Mrs. Otis A. Warner, Mrs. Charles E. Webb, Mrs. Charles D. Burrell, Mrs. Ross DeMuth, Miss Martha La Van, Mrs. George M. Wilson and Mrs. Roy Smithers.

Much later, the Rossford Business and Professional Women's Club was organized, with charter presentation in charge of Mrs. Hester Wickens, president of the Ohio Federation of B and PW Clubs, and Mrs. Thelma Nehring, president of the Toledo B and PW Club.

The old Peck & May boat yard beside Grassy creek, taken about 1908. Many sleek catboats were built there, along with the Walbridge Park "Arawana." Note the old "long legged" wood supports for the bridge in left background, where today traffic zooms up the hill toward Perrysburg.

Contractor Fred Rinker, who built many homes in Rossford, and his son, Frank, on his knee. Frank married Ella Uffmann, sister of Fred Uffmann, Jr.

First officers of the Rossford group: Mrs. Alice Appt, president; Mrs. Emma Warner, vice president; Miss Florence Watters, secretary; Mrs. Isabel Heinemann, treasurer.

* * *

What's a Pot House diploma? That may not be a fair question, since only one was ever presented.

Earl W. White, veteran maker of clay pots, presented it one day to George Ross Ford, Jr. (now a member of the board of directors) after George completed a stint in the old clay pot house at Rossford.

Inasmuch as George rode a motorcycle to work in those days, the somewhat elaborate scroll was very appropriate—a sketch of a lad riding a white motor-cycle, with a dinner pail over his shoulder.

Mr. White, who was a pot house man in the early glass days of Findlay, Ohio, and who later saw service at Crystal City, Missouri, Tarentum, Pennsylvania, Kokomo, Indiana, was the father of Gerald White.

Jerry, as most people call him, began in the Rossford pot house back in 1921. He became associated later with George Ford Jr. in several experimental activities at Rossford. He rose to a plant superintendency, specialties division, and more recently became head of an important new Plant Development section at Rossford.

He married Genevieve Lewis, daughter of William Lewis, Rossford veteran.

* * *

George Ross Ford, Sr. was a very disgruntled young man one day in 1905, when his father told him to get ready to take a pleasure trip to Mexico.

Mr. and Mrs. Edward Ford, with other Toledoans, had arranged to take advantage of the then new idea of a Pullman vacation trip to Mexico—living and dining aboard. The trips began and ended in Chicago.

George insisted he would die on such a trip, pointing out how seasick and nauseated street cars and trains made him.

Father Ford was adamant, so George found himself in Chicago, watching the trains coming in from many

points to join the special Pullman party for Mexico.

A young lady got off the Detroit train. After one look at her, 23-year-old George forgot all about the possibility of getting seasick on the Mexican trip. He casually followed her into the big station, saw to his delighted amazement that she and her parents walked right up to Mr. and Mrs. Edward Ford. The elders exchanged cordial greetings. George joined the group.

That's how he met the girl that became his wife Grace Miller, daughter of Sherman R. Miller. (The latter, as a youth, had worked for D. M. Ferry of Detroit, whose seed company became internationally famous. Mr. Ferry married Mr. Miller's sister.)

With the glow of candlelight in her eyes, Mrs. Ford looked into the long ago as she said, a ghost of a smile on her face: "When I came to Toledo for an occasional visit, George always met me at the old Milburn Wagon Works railway station on Monroe street in Auburndale. It seems like he always had a different automobile—racy things that frightened me."

George Ford and Grace Miller were married February 22, 1907, two days after her 23rd birthday.

* * *

Daniel H. Startsman, president of William Glenny Glass of Cincinnati, likes to recall a visit to Edward Ford

Left: Tom Wood, one of Rossford's pioneers much thought of by everyone. He was a dog lover, a great hunter.

Right: Mrs. Tom Wood. 72

Plate in the early days, right after George Ross Ford became president.

Dan was desperately in need of four carloads of glass, but could get only two. There were shortages at the time, and he knew it, but he had made a special trip to argue personally.

The sales manager, Roy Helm, was adamant, explaining that it was against policy. As he got up to leave, his face showing his disappointment, Dan saw George Ford approaching. They had been friends for years and greeted each other heartily, ending with Ford asking Startsman why he was looking so down in the mouth. Dan explained.

Mr. Ford stared at the floor for a moment, then said to Helm, "Let Dan have the four cars."

The sales manager protested, pointing out that Ford himself had set the rigid policy for the duration of the shortage.

"Sometimes," George Ford replied slowly, "it is difficult to stick to a rigid policy. Many years ago, my grandfather, Capt. Ford, was desperately in need of cash. Mr. Startsman's grandfather loaned him $10,000. No papers were signed. They just shook hands. That's why I think Dan ought to have those four cars—don't you think so, Roy?"

Helm glared at the ground, scratched his head, then grinned. "Yeah, I guess you're right."

* * *

The Liedigk family has a long, long service record in glass.

Joseph, who brought his family from Germany, worked in Creighton, and came early to Rossford—the whole family riding in a freight car with Joe's two cows, furniture and a cat and a dog.

Frank, a son, born in Germany, 1885, began at Creighton when he was 11, as a water boy—two wooden buckets balanced by a shoulder support. Later he threw rouge on the glass to be polished.

Frank lives at 139 Hannum avenue. The youngest brother, Paul, lives at 134 Jennings road, and Gus, another brother, also lives on Jennings road. There are two glass-working nephews, Hubert and Anthony, both of 144 Windsor Drive.

* * *

There's no brighter thread in the pattern of Rossford than the Strickers.

The Liedigk (pronounced Leedick) brothers, representing some 200 years of employment, were featured in a national magazine some few years ago for their combined years of service with the Fords. Left to right: Paul, 1907; Frank, 1899; August and Joseph, 1899.

Anna Stricker, wife of veteran Joe Mainz, came from Germany in 1891 with her mother and five brothers, to join other German families who settled in Creighton after hearing from Capt. Ford.

Three of her brothers, Philip, Frank and Tony worked in the Ford plant at Creighton; Felix came with his family to Rossford to work, too, as Edward Ford got under way. Felix married a daughter of Bart Schmitz, a Ford City glass worker; Tony married Catherine Bayer, an aunt of veteran Jake Bayer.

Philip, Anna's eldest brother, married Margaret Straub, whose romance was promoted by Capt. Ford himself—in the great kitchen of his home at Creighton. Margaret cooked for the Old Captain for many years.

Anna also cooked, but for Artemus Pitcairn, cousin of John Pitcairn, with whom the Fords had the big fall-out years later. (Artemus and the Fords always remained on friendly terms.)

Anna's sister worked at the Artemus Pitcairn home, too. Artemus had nine children, and Mrs. Pitcairn used to work in the kitchen with Anna (then 16) to supervise and help with the huge meals.

"My, but those were exciting, wonderful times," recalls Anna Mainz. "The Edward Ford and Emory Ford families used to come there often for dinner . . . but Mr. Pitcairn had plenty of room, a big house and 40 acres in woods, an orchard and usually a big field of sweet corn."

* * *

Sixty-three years after her marriage in 1893, Margaret (Straub) Stricker, just a wisp of a little old lady, well remembered her girlhood, when she cooked for Capt. John B. Ford.

"When my husband was courting me, Capt. Ford always seemed to know when he was coming to see me. He would place two chairs close together in the kitchen, and then sneak away." (Phil, who worked in the packing department at the Creighton plant, died in Rossford in 1934.)

"Yes," said Mrs. Stricker in reply to a question, "Capt. Ford was a pretty good eater. He used to buy pork chop tenderloins almost every day for his breakfast.

"He always came out into the kitchen quite early of a morning. He'd take the big tea-kettle of hot water and make himself a hot toddy . . . called it his medicine.

"He'd have fruit juice, eggs and his pork chop tenderloins. I usually made hot biscuits for him every morning. He would pile on the butter, and then load his knife with my plum preserves and put that on top of the butter. He used to buy the plums from Artemus Pitcairn for me to make into preserves."

Mrs. Stricker's eyes twinkled as she recalled Capt. Ford's wedding gift to her.

"I was terribly embarrassed when I opened it. I can still hear Capt. Ford, grinning as he scowled at me, say: 'Now Maggie, that'll come in handy one of these days.'

"It was beautiful—a white cashmere baby's coat and cape. . . . I used it for all of my ten children."

* * *

There's no "Englisher" name than Tom Brown. Let's unravel Tom's family string. It reaches clear across the Atlantic to Rossford.

Tom's father, Arthur, was a plate glass man in England (Pilkington). He moved to America. Tom became a kiln dresser for Capt. Ford at Creighton, moved to Rossford in 1901 to be with his old boss, Edward Ford.

Two of Tom's brothers, Walter and Ernest, came along from England, too, worked as stripping yard men for the Fords.

Tom died in Rossford in 1917. That was two years after one of Tom's sons, Herb Brown, began at Rossford.

Herb began in the carpenter shop under Sam Mannell, Sr., Ed Ford's right hand bower for many years. (Sam worked for the Fords for 45 years before retiring.)

Herb worked in the office for awhile, back into the factory, and now is foreman in the edging department, automotive. He married Mabel Lewis, one of the six children of Mr. and Mrs. William Lewis, who came on

Scenes when they began construction work on
No. 2 plant in 1911. No. 2 began operating in 1913.

Looking down center span of grinding
and polishing building (May 27, 1911).

Lower end of grinding and polishing building (May 27, 1911)

with so many families to Rossford after the big fire and
flood in Valley Park, Missouri, in 1916.

Three of Herb's brothers-in-law: Earl Lewis of Toledo
Plate & Window Glass Company; Robert, a teacher at
Scott High; and Kenneth Lewis, in the wareroom
at Rossford.

Herb's sister-in-law, Genevieve Lewis, married Gerald
White, long associated with the Rossford plant.

Herb's wife, Mabel, was the telephone operator during
the flood and holocaust at Valley Park. Last to leave
her post, Mabel was removed by boat.

Speaking of the Valley Park disaster which brought so
many families to Rossford, none could recall it more
vividly than George Miller, a G & P man at Rossford
and who served as fire chief at Rossford. The flood was
on his father's birthday, necessitating a postponement of
the party, while invited guests got busy rescuing men,
women and children from second-floor windows.

This picture, made by fitting two side by side to get the
over all scene, is believed to have been taken about 1913.
Note the No. 2 plant casting hall, background left. The
middle background is now almost solid with buildings,
the huge sand pile re-located. At far right are the old rough
storage building and, closer, the start of the wareroom
that includes part of today's operation.

75

THE FOUR PHILBINS—William H. Philbin, far right, labor superintendent, 1900-1917; to his right, Bill Philbin, his son, who succeeded Bill, 1917 to 1946; next to Bill, his son, Phil, and Phil's son, Phil, Jr. . . . four generations.

In Rossford's alphabet, P stands for Philbin. And well it might.

The late Phil Philbin, a teamster in the early days for A. Bentley & Sons, is believed to be the first man ever transferred from the Bentley payroll to the Fords'.

He became labor superintendent, 1906 to 1917. His son, William A., worked under carpenter foreman Sam Mannell, Sr., who had been with the Fords since the days of Louisville and Jeffersonville.

William retired some years ago.

William's son, Philip A., began at Rossford in 1918. Today he is in charge of freight traffic, in and out; the big unloading cranes and in charge of general service and maintenance for such operations. His brother, William Wade Philbin, works with him.

Philip A. Philbin, Jr., representing the fourth generation, is in production control at Rossford.

Bill Philbin recalled an incident about Capt. Ford.

"It happened one morning in the spring of 1899. (Philbin was 18 then, the Old Captain 88.) I didn't know the old gentleman personally, but I knew who he was, of course.

"I came around a corner—it was about 7 o'clock in the morning—and there sitting on a keg of nails was the old gentleman. He glared at me, then in his gruff voice asked: 'Bill, where's Edward?'

"I was so surprised that he knew my name that I couldn't think of an answer, and before I could reply the Old Captain growled: 'Huh, I came all the way up from Pennsylvanie. I'm here. *I'm* here—where's Edward. He's late.'

"I was scared. And I got t'hell outta there."

How early did Edward Ford get on the job?

Otto Johnson, first a coachman and then a chauffeur for President Ford, has an interesting answer.

"I had standing orders to be at the carriage block in front of the residence (2205 Collingwood avenue) at 8 a.m."

Otto recalls that Mr. Ford's first automobile was an electric, and that one, a brougham, steered from the top. . . . Otto recalls, too, that much earlier Mr. Ford had "two high-stepping bays."

Born in Sweden, Otto passed his 85th milestone in 1956. His wife, Mina Killgus, born in Stuttgart, Germany, came to this country all alone when she was 17. That was in 1897. She worked in the Edward Ford household for many years.

Well, look who's here, posing in 1910. Left to right: Foreman Ed Brown, Fred Heide and Dick Grimes; top: Fred Richards and Dyke Westfall.

Memories of the Edward Ford Plate Glass Company Rossford Band remain as a loving memory in the minds of many citizens. World War I took many of its members; some of the players have passed on, but many still were active in 1956.

The band played in many places, provided stirring music for those trips to Sugar Island when Ford management chartered the steamer Greyhound for an employee outing. Here is the roster of the 46-piece band as it was listed for a program in Rossford High auditorium on February 22, 1917, when C. H. Smith was conductor:

Hubert Vanderkool	cornet	Grant Sarver	bassoon
Riley Finch	cornet	Irving Westfall	flute
B. Drake	cornet	Frank Stricker	flute
Peter Beuth	cornet	George Purcell, Sr.	saxoph.
Al Logan	cornet	Orville Doren	saxoph.
Herbert Henlein	cornet	Ira Rook	saxoph.
A. Thompson	cornet	Earl Sarver	saxoph.
Howard Carson	cornet	William King	saxoph.
Bart Stricker	cornet	George Purcell, Jr.	saxoph.
Peter Luyet	cornet	A. Lyrtack	saxoph.
Emil Ferry	clarinet	William Stricker	horn
Henry Beitry	clarinet	Portus Felise	horn
Harry Fuller	clarinet	James Talliere	horn
Dr. L. J. Herold	clarinet	J. Hote	horn
Livingston Holst	clarinet	H. Charles	trombone
W. D. Durliat	clarinet	A. Porter	trombone
V. Bena	clarinet	Joe Purcell	trombone
Harold Carson	clarinet	Felix Stricker	trombone
Thomas Bardett	clarinet	Glenn Doren	trombone
Tony Stricker	clarinet	Frank Krakau	trombone
M. Foltz	clarinet	S. Holkoupc	trombone
George Daysley	clarinet	L. Van Pelt	drum
J. Sanko	clarinet	R. Bettis	drum and traps

Emil Ferry, a finisher in the casting hall, had played in a Belgian army band. While resting from his labors, he played his clarinet in the old casting hall. Emil led the band after Mr. Smith resigned.

Educational note: J. A. Shriver, principal of the old Walnut Street School (Rossford's first) created a sensation among some Rossford parents when he wanted their children to try reading after school hours . . . there was consternation when Morrison R. Van Cleve, later to become a well known naturalist and biologist, came to Rossford and tried, as principal, to get pupils interested in the study of bugs, toads and flowers.

One father, however, after long consideration of the problem, eased the concern of some of the puzzled foreign-born parents by saying: "Well, now maybe it would make the kids think of something beside upsetting our back-houses."

* * *

Who was the jumpingest Jump Center the Rossford club basketball fans watched in the early 1920's?

Two oldtimers, Jake Bayer and Herb Brown, were both asked the question, but not when they were together. Both had the same answer, with grins: "That would be Junie MacNichol."

* * *

Ival Gale Fowler

Ival Gale Fowler. But just call him Tige. He was the first graduate engineer to arrive on the Rossford scene after David H. Goodwillie was hired as chief engineer soon after President Edward Ford's death.

Tige is a native of Fowlerville, Michigan, (named for one of his relatives) 25 miles east of Lansing.

After graduating in the sanitary branch of civil engineering at Michigan, Tige drifted to Toledo where some of his classmates already were at work under Mr. Goodwillie, then Service Director of Toledo. Mr. Goodwillie put him to work.

Look ma, two telephones. And your magnifying glass will disclose Electrician Fred Halford's button shoes. And look—Pin Up art, too, on the wall of Fred's office.

Joe Henry was paymaster at the start, and for many years.

After a stint in World War I, Tige was back in Toledo, doing about the same work, but for a New York firm, Fuller & McClintock, retained by Mr. Goodwillie when he became service director and acting water commissioner.

Tige likes to recall the expression on the face of Mr. Goodwillie when he returned to the office one day, following a talk with W. W. Knight, then a vice president and a director of Edward Ford Plate. They had been at a city franchise evaluation committee meeting together, and were walking along Superior street in Toledo.

"Goodwillie's eyes were popping when he came into the office," said Fowler in recalling it. Mr. Goodwillie related that Mr. Knight had just offered him a position as chief engineer at "that glass plant across the river."

"He offered me a salary of $10,000 to start," Mr. Goodwillie had said. "Ten thousand dollars, Tige . . . and I don't know one dam' thing about glass."

ROSSFORD'S FIRST 30-YEAR CLUB

		Started
Warren Davis	138 Bacon st.	1899
Joseph Mainz	231 Hannum ave.	1899
A. Liedigk	144 Jennings rd.	1899
F. Liedigk	139 Hannum ave.	1899
Walter Walker	327 White st., Toledo	1901
George Becker	933 Mulberry st., Perrysburg	1901
James King	208 Dixie Terrace	1902
Irving Richards	170 Hannum ave.	1902
Joseph Rossler	407 Superior st.	1902
John Klepacz	137 Bacon st.	1903
William Langendonk	141 Bacon st.	1904
Michael Szczeparski	715 E. Hudson st., Toledo	1904
Adam Jerry (Gyori)	132 Helen dr.	1904
Peter Ignaczak	Route No. 3, Perrysburg	1905
Steve Kotowski	556 E. Indiana ave., Perrysburg	1907
Michael Cieply	220 Hannum ave.	1907
Paul Liedigk	134 Jennings rd.	1907
Leo Winkler	435 Hayes rd., Toledo	1908
John Henning	5796 Stewart rd., Sylvania	1908
Sam Nail	183 Oak st.	1908
Charles Badik	210 Colony rd.	1908
Thomas Hatas	Route No. 3, Perrysburg	1908
Frank Dudek	225 Elm st.	1909
Paul Chipley (Cieply)	503 Beech st.	1909
John Stackowicz	200 Elm st.	1909
John Knurek	168 Bergen st.	1909

FIRST ROSSFORD FOREMEN

William Philbin	East River rd., Perrysburg	1899–Labor
John Scharf	578 Yondota st., Toledo	1899–Brickmason
Jacob Suidyla	120 E. Central, Toledo	1900–Grinder
Harvey P. Gampher	121 Eagle Pt. rd.	1901–Casting Hall
Charles Brown	212 Dixie Hwy., Rossford	1902–Stores
Henry Beuth	Windsor dr., Rossford	1907–Casting Hall
Charles Burrell	116 Eagle Pt. rd.	1909–Carpenter

The following were casting hall foremen, in order of their names, from 1900 to 1930:

Jeff Venable, Joe Smith and John King, all before and right after 1900.

Beginning in 1904: Theodore Paffrath, John Schiffgen, August Shoele, Gene Toumison, William Furlong, Eric Brown.

Albert Fair, Dan Mogel, August Shubert, Alex Gallagher, William Weber, Sr., Harvey Gampher, Henry J. Beuth and William Rager.

CHAPTER 12

The Old and The New

When he became president of his father's glass works in 1920 at the age of 38, George Ross Ford, Sr. had the advantage of remembering the crude production days of 1898, and all the improvements made in the 22 intervening years.

As a 16-year-old, he was on hand when they christened the new sand barge as "The City of Rossford" in 1898, watched it slide into the inlet from the river where it had been loaded with grinding sand, watched them unload with a crude trolley system of buckets.

When it was found that the river sand was too soft for glass-grinding purposes, George had watched them extend the railroad spur so that cars of sand from Lake Michigan dunes could be brought in. And he knew the first names of the 16 strapping lads who wheel-barrowed the grinding sand (about 300 pounds per load) some 400 feet to the grinding department, at twelve and one-half cents an hour.

When those same huskies gathered at noon to play baseball, George coaxed them to let him play. With sly winks at each other, they always would say: "Well, George, maybe you could—if we had some chawin' tobacco." And the response was always the same — George sprinting across the pasture to a store, racing back with pockets stuffed with bags of Mail Pouch and Blue Hen, and Star Plug.

George could remember when continuous lehrs were first tried, how they out-dated the periodic kilns, reducing annealing time from three days to three hours; how this led to larger grinding and polishing tables, and how this all helped to improve the quality of the glass, and greatly expand production.

He watched them start construction on Plant No. 2 in 1911, and was on hand for the first cast in 1913. He was 31 now, and taking an active part in the office end of the business.

Buddies. George Ross Ford and Clark E. Husted were almost constantly together for 56 years, dating from the time Clark joined Edward Ford Plate.

Early office force and key men. Seated on grass, left to right: Mert Perry, Mary Thraves, Van Hudepohl, Ida McGlone, Cy Taylor, Miss Baker, George Saelzer, William Rumbaugh, Jennie Dawson and Roy Lewis.
Second row: Mr. Keller, Claude Lewis, George D. DeMaid, George R. Ford, Harry Cochran, Kuhms, Clark Husted, Joe Henry.
Third row: Sam Mannel, George Henderson, Edward King, Vincent Fildes, John Mogul, Jim Blake, Fred Halstead and Fred Halford.
Back row: Henry Hohl, John King, Frank Krakau, Alex Gallagher, Walter King.

He had watched the booming plant slow down as World War I got under way, and, knowing every worker, often went with Jake Bayer to make the rounds of homes to check on the welfare of families whose men his father had been forced to lay off.

Finally, as president after his father's death, George Ford, Sr., welcomed the introduction of skilled engineers and other new faces, sensing the great new possibilities ahead, and personally intrigued by the market potential for the skyrocketing young automotive industry.

Years before, George had begged his father to build an automobile plant on the high ground bordering Grassy Creek; he was blissfully unaware that father knew all about his little experimental shop in a far corner of the plant, or that father knew about the time George had shown, in secret, his blueprint for a new type of automobile engine to Band Leader Smith. And, too, George had coaxed his father to buy the Overland Auto plant.

An automobile engine throbbed in his heart, but George Ford was proud of his plate glass heritage, and as the leader now,

he heartily welcomed any plan that would improve Operations Rossford.

He was delighted, for example, when Chief Engineer Goodwillie introduced a young man not long out of the University of Michigan—the first graduate engineer Mr. Goodwillie hired after he went to Rossford. The chap's name was I. G. Fowler.

When he reported for duty on February 15, 1923, Tige Fowler was instructed to make a survey of the factory area. He drew up an accurately-scaled map of water and sewer lines, talking to oldtimers to locate many of them, often digging to find forgotten pipelines.

Soon the pressure of new plant engineering activities almost forced the abandonment of the survey, but it was kept up so that information could be added as needed.

Dinner group at the Bull Dog Cafe, St. Clair and Jackson streets. Left to right, in front: Mr. O'Dwyer, father-in-law of Harry Cochran; Jim Bake and Ed King.
Left to right, standing: Jack Whitmore, Bill King, Dick Hazlett, Mart Callahan, Charles and Harvey Gampher, waiter, next unknown, and another waiter.
Seated, clockwise: Alex Gallagher, Bert Henderson, John Scharf, Vincent Fildes, Sam Mannel, John King, Frank Krakau, Don Mogel, and Henry Hohl.

That was a new touch of modern engineering. No guessing.

Mr. Goodwillie's first improvement, when he arrived a few years earlier, had been the installation of pyrometers on the pot furnaces, something of an insult to the oldtimers who had trained eyes to gauge the temperature of glass.

But that was, at best, guess work. And so the old time rule-of-thumb methods began to fade before the bristling intrusion of draft gauges, combustion control intruments and automatic stokers. There was much wagging of heads and argument among the older boys as Chief Engineer Goodwillie persuaded management to buy its coal by BTU content, to take full advantage of high fusion point and low ash content.

These pioneering developments of the new era of scientific procedure, crude as they were in comparison to today's electronic age, marked a sharp departure, however, from the early days of plate glass manufacture in America.

Then a factory was practically a one-man organization. The key man was the plant superintendent. He had his own pet ideas, carried his own recipes, secret glass batch formulas, clay mixtures for the pots, emery and rouge processing notes.

Most of this information was carried in his head, some of it in note books he kept locked in his desk or at home, in case he was moved to a new location, or was hired by a rival manufacturer. It was not unusual for a glass plant superintendent to take most of the key men with him whenever he made a new connection. The majority of such men had been trained by their father or some relative; the batch man kept his own counsel, as did the polisher, the grinder, the skimmer and teemer.

America had not yet grown its own crop of chemists in those early days, and few had come in from European industrial centers; none such talent was available to pioneering American glassmen, even had they wanted to avail themselves of it; university-trained engineers and technicians were a rarity.

Whenever advice was needed to install a piece of new equipment, often reluctantly accepted and viewed with

They didn't charge extra for Roquefort cheese in those days.

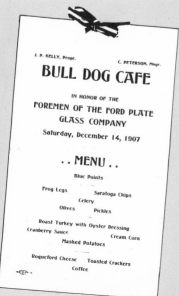

J. P. KELLY, Propr.   C. PETERSON, Mngr.

BULL DOG CAFE

IN HONOR OF THE
FOREMEN OF THE FORD PLATE
GLASS COMPANY

Saturday, December 14, 1907

.. MENU ..

Blue Points

Frog Legs   Saratoga Chips
                Celery
        Olives   Pickles

Roast Turkey with Oyster Dressing
Cranberry Sauce
                    Cream Corn
        Mashed Potatoes

Roqueford Cheese   Toasted Crackers
            Coffee

"That Old Gang of Mine." Ed Connelly, George Ford, Bill Scharf, Gene Kimmell, Mr. Eckenrode, sales manager; Herb Heinline, Vern Evans (checkered cap), Roland Beers.

Seven Sweeties of the good old days. Can you identify any of them?

Clyde King, left; Luella Woodward, Elizabeth Thornton, Max Wood and Jimmy LeRoy.

suspicion, the makers of the equipment were required by the glass factory owners to provide all technical services, and then depart from the sacred grounds on tip-toe.

This secretiveness, refusal to transmit information and reluctance to try new things combined with suspicion of suggestions of new ideas and techniques by outsiders, often led to only one thing—stagnation. The smaller plant owners were the greatest offenders, and they either passed out of existence when their superintendent died, or were purchased by the more progressive groups.

Capt. Ford had prospered because progress was his meat. He had dared to use gas, and thus revolutionized methods of glass melt; he had broken the European monopoly on soda ash, the plate glass industry's most important ingredient.

George Ross Ford, son and grandson of those illustrious pioneers of "let's do it a better way," wanted a better road, too—one that skirted the pools of stagnation and dirt roads of the horse 'n' buggy-minded.

The enormous strides made at Rossford by planned research, experiment and development in the 1920-1930 decade of George Ross Ford's reign cannot be fully appreciated unless compared with the two decades preceding.

The one furnace of 1898 could melt 20 small pots of glass, each containing about 1000 pounds. The pots were made within the plant by men whose trade was handed down from father to son. After drying, the pots were burned in pot kilns to prepare them for melting their glass ingredients in the furnace.

In lieu of piping natural gas from a distance, fuel for melting was producer gas (made by burning coal under conditions which produced a combustible gas, but of low heat value).

Crude methods were used to transfer the pots of molten glass from the furnaces to the iron casting table, where the pot was emptied by hand operations. A cast-iron roller was pulled across the glass to flatten it, the pulling force being a hand-operated winch. After the molten mass had been flattened into a rough sheet or plate glass blank, it was hand-lifted and placed in kilns for annealing, a three-day process.

(Later methods enabled workmen to shove the blanks into a series of ovens, then finally to a semi-continuous lehr where the glass was cooled by lowering temperatures at intervals . . . Edward Ford Plate was the first factory to have built for it and to successfully operate a continuous lehr, it having been developed at the Marsh Plate Glass Company machine-equipment factory in Floreffe, Pennsylvania, marking a radical reduction in annealing time, from three days to three hours. And better annealing was accomplished.)

The rough blanks were transferred from the annealing department to iron grinder tables 24 feet in diameter, where they were again handled by hand methods. Matchers, men expert in fast calculation by eye, determined the most efficient amount of glass that could be placed upon a given table by noting the various sizes of rough blanks (often broken into smaller pieces by accident after leaving the lehr).

After grinding, the glass was turned over for grinding the other side. After that the ground glass was polished on both sides.

Ladies Aid Society of Rossford Methodist Church, at 1902 outing in Walbridge Park: Front row, seated, left to right: Flora Kier, Dan Harris, Priscilla Pepper, George Henry, Unknown, Sadie Zerney.
Second row: Mrs. May Hufford and son Robert. Unknown, Mrs. John L. Henry, Ethel Stocking, Mrs. Frank Krakau, Sr., Jennie Warner, William King, Unknown, Mrs. Martin, William Tracey, Mrs. Ross Tuller, Mrs. Oscar Holts, Mrs. Matthias R. Pepper, Sr., Mrs. Zerney, Mrs. Thomas Brown, Mrs. Austin Tracy, Mr. Austin Tracy.
Third row: Mrs. John Shoecraft, Mr. Elliott Warner, Mrs. Westfall, Mrs. Arthur Harris, Mrs. Curry, Mrs. Pritchard, Mrs. Cook, Merel Stocking, Lillian Pepper, Jennie Kier, Mrs. Chas. Kier, Mrs. Stebbins, Unknown, Mrs. Chas. Harris, Unknown, Mrs. William Tracey, Mrs. William Harris, Unknown, Mrs. John Connors, Mrs. Elliot Warner.

Rossford fire department, 1925. On fender, left: Tom Crawford; above him, Merrill Steward; back of Merrill, William Brown; on seat at left, Emory (Dyke) Westfall, Clarence Sawyer and Bill Langevin.

In front, beside fender: Mr. Gorka, back him, Orvel Doren, and to his left, Roy Steward. On seat, left to right, Bill Sevenish, Chief Ed Brown and Earl Corbin. (Chief Brown and his son were electrocuted in a fire at the John Caple mills.)

Plant No. 1, with certain improvements in 1901 and subsequent years, featuring the use of electricity for power about 1907, reached a production peak of slightly more than five and one-half million square feet annually near the end of its 13-year operational period.

Plant No. 2 was begun late in 1911, the first cast made in 1913. This completely new unit was near the old factory, but many, many improvements and enlargements were designed into its facilities by Edward Ford and his associates, including a study of straight line production flow, and installation of certain improvements along those channels.

The circular clay pots were doubled in size, so that each could hold a ton of glass. Gas producers were improved. Furnaces were enlarged and overhead electrically-operated cranes installed for more efficient pot transportation. And mechanical motor-driven devices were installed to improve handling of the pouring and teeming (emptying onto the casting table) of the glass.

A larger casting table was installed to handle the greater amounts of glass from the bigger pots, and the annealing lehr was enlarged to take care of the larger rough blanks. The newer lehr was semi-automatic in operation, again improving the annealing of the product.

Hand-operated overhead conveyors were installed to carry the blanks to the grinder units, eliminating many accidents to men by the hand-carrying methods.

The grinding and polishing tables were enlarged to 36-foot diameter affairs, so that each could hold 1,000 square feet of glass; and the grinder and polisher heads had to be newly designed. Power drives for them were directly connected to large motors, whereas the older machines had long leather belts, a constant threat to life or limb.

Semi-automatic devices were installed to transport grinding sand from the big outdoor pile to the grinders—ending the era of wheel-barrow transportation.

A new power house was built to accommodate steam turbines for electrical generation, replacing the steam engines of the old plant; additional railroad trackage, sewers, deep wells, new plaster, batch and rouge houses and an emery-grading plant were all a part of this new expansion.

Thus did the new replace the old and the new of 1912 become increasingly obsolete in the Roaring Twenties.

There came that first wave of improvements begun when Mr. Goodwillie came upon the scene in 1920, followed by Tige Fowler in the summer of 1923.

Before the end of that year, management decided to expand operations by adding a second pot-casting layout, with a new rod-type lehr; two additional 36-foot round polishing tables and one additional 36-foot grinder, along with four more pot-melting furnaces, and newer automatic gas producers for melting.

Huge 36-foot tables replaced the old-time 24 footers for grinding and polishing plate glass at Rossford. Note the workman, far right, for a comparison in size. Such tables were used right up to the time when a continuous grinding and polishing line was installed in the late Twenties.

Engineering for all this was done largely by Messrs. Goodwillie, Fowler and plant engineer Platt, with assistance from A. Bentley & Sons and Hoover, Owens & Rentscheler of Hamilton, Ohio, whose engineers had made foundation sketches for the existing grinding and polishing departments.

On the Rossford scene at that time was a hard-working young college engineer, with the Bentleys during his vacations. His name was William H. Hasselbach.

It would develop that he would spend other vacations there, loaned by Bentley to the Fords. Who could tell? He just might become a permanent part of this glass scene some day.

The year 1926 was a big one. Veteran Platt, with an ailing heart, departed for Florida, and Tige Fowler replaced him. (Mr. Platt died later that year.) New engineering talent was being sought, and outside consultants brought in—Ralph Gram of Langdon, Hohly & Gram, for the reinforced concrete of the big new batch house, and others.

Harold Schutz, an expert in bottle machine design engineering, was hired to study a new pot-casting device, the Bicheroux machine, in use in Germany at the time. He went to Germany in company with Mr. and Mrs. Goodwillie and Mr. and Mrs. Clark Husted.

H. E. Robinson was employed to assist in an improved design for a contemplated Ford-operated Bicheroux casting method, along with accessory changes that would be necessary, both in furnace and lehr adaptations. E. L. Walters, another engineer, was brought in to add to needed engineering personnel.

James B. Haworth, a Purdue engineering graduate, was hired to study and supervise operations of the new gas producers, and other production problems.

By 1928, investigation was under way for the first continuous grinding and polishing line operation to replace the individual roundtable grinders and polishers that had served the industry for so long.

Messrs. Goodwillie and Fowler were sent to Europe to study continuous G and P methods that had been introduced there. They visited plants in Germany, France, Belgium and England.

(Tige Fowler will never forget his visit to the office of Max Bicheroux, wealthy German industrialist and big game hunter, at Herzogenrath, 12 miles from the great glass works at Aachen, from where so many Ford men had come in the long ago . . . in a pen back of his office, Mr. Bicheroux kept a wild boar!)

Messrs. Goodwillie and Fowler met John B. Ford in Brussels, where he was staying at the time, while investigating the Heuze continuous grinding and polishing method which Rossford management planned to be used with the semi-automatic Bicheroux machine.

Mr. Ford, still first vice president of Edward Ford Plate at the time, although heading the alkali operations in Wyandotte, was a friend of Charles Heuze, Sr., of the firm of Heuze, Malevez & Simon, manufacturers of glass-making machinery, and, oddly enough it seems, producers of chocolate-making machines and equipment to polish marble.

Messrs. Ford, Goodwillie and Fowler went to the Heuze plant at Auvelais, Belgium, 40 miles southeast of Brussels. (They had lunch at Namur, where Tige, as a World War I veteran, recalled that the Germans had shot hundreds of Belgians and dumped them into the little Namur river.)

After being assured by Mr. Goodwillie that the Bicheroux machine being operated experimentally for the company in Germany would work satisfactorily, Mr. Ford authorized Mr. Goodwillie to deposit a certified check with Heuze, Malevez & Simon to confirm that Edward Ford Plate was now ready to have HMS begin construction of the huge machinery that would be shipped overseas to Rossford, inaugurating another great advance.

And so the new faces came in. John Townsend, among other engineers, in 1929. And, oh, yes—over in that ditch there being excavated for the coming of the great new G and P lines—the young fellow with the spade. Why that's George Ross Ford, Jr. Shades of his great grandfather, the Old Captain, who in cutaway coat and high silk hat, had often jumped into a trench when they were excavating for foundations for the Ford City plant almost 40 years before. There was one slight difference . . . George didn't chew tobacco.

Production possibilities undreamed of a few decades before were rapidly approaching practical realism.

In 1870, when Capt. Ford was America's only plate glass manufacturer, annual production was 120,000 square feet. Bankrupt footage.

Stimulated by Capt. Ford's startling comeback on the banks of the Allegheny, production rose in 1890 to 10,500,000 square feet—equal to eighty percent of American consumption of plate glass that year. The Old Warrior, despite hell and high water, and an inadequate tariff, had helped to reduce imports to a point where the folk across the ocean had only twenty percent of the American business.

In another year, right when they were unveiling the statue at Ford City, America had eleven plate glass plants—seven in Pennsylvania, three in Indiana and one in Missouri.

In 1920, when Edward Ford Plate Glass began to build great new wings for a spectacular production flight, total plate glass output in the United States had reached 50,000,000 square feet.

Exactly 20 years before, Edward Ford Plate produced about 1,100,000 square feet in its first full year of 1900; increased by about 600,000 square feet the following year. In 1902, with the Works fully equipped, shipments totaled more than 2,700,000 square feet.

By 1910, just before construction started on larger Plant No. 2, production reached 4,643,309 square feet annually; by 1915, with the second plant going full tilt, production soared to 5,709,106 square feet. By 1920, it was 9,326,582 square feet—approximately one-fifth of all plate glass produced in the United States that year.

Edward Ford Plate ranked high in production facilities among the country's six plate glass manufacturers by 1926.

American Plate at Kane, Pennsylvania, had eight furnaces, with 160 pots; Ford Motor, with three plants, had eight furnaces and 128 pots; National Plate, also with three plants, had 31 furnaces and 620 pots; Pittsburgh Plate Glass, with the greatest number of plants (six) had 44 furnaces and 676 pots; Standard Plate, with two plants had eight furnaces and 160 pots while Edward Ford Plate had 16 furnaces and 320 pots—largest pots-per-plant operation in the United States.

There were high hopes at Rossford, therefore, when experiments with the new Bicheroux machine disclosed that, whereas the method in use gave the grinding table a sheet of glass from $\frac{1}{2}$ to $\frac{9}{16}$ of an inch thick (to be ground to $\frac{1}{4}$ inch thinness,) the newer machine could cast the rough blank much thinner for grinding.

The Bicheroux, with its big water-cooled iron rollers, would control thickness *before* the glass reached the casting table. The rollers, squeezing the glass through much like a clothes wringer, could be set to pre-determine the thickness desired.

This method would save a lot of grinding time, eliminate much of the costly wear on equipment, and make it possible to utilize more glass per pot, instead of losing so much by grinding, and by breakage incident to the current method.

The Bicheroux machine was placed in operation on July 14, 1928, casting for the round tables until the start of the new continuous and polishing lines in June of 1930.

The Bicheroux-round table method increased production to 14,191,515 square feet in 1929.

This was the year, incidentally, when that promising

William H. Hasselbach

young engineer, Bill Hasselbach, who had been loaned to the Fords by Bentley Construction in his college vacations of 1923 and 1924, became a member of the expanding Edward Ford Plate engineering staff on a full-time basis. (Mr. Hasselbach had graduated from the University of Michigan in 1926. He returned to Rossford on a full-time basis in 1927, on the Bentley payroll, but on July 1, 1929, he was employed full-time by Edward Ford Plate.)

Vast new capital had been required for the immense improvement in facilities, and there was one special arrangement that might well have made the Old Captain roar with anger. The slides or tracks upon which the tables of glass moved forward under the grinders and polishers were of English design; the oscillating grinder heads were of German design, the polisher units of French design!

Thus, basic patent rights for one production line operation were purchased from developments in three different European countries—another reason why just anybody cannot have a plate glass plant in his own backyard.

Everybody's backyard, incidentally, became overgrown with the weeds of worry as the most shocking financial sandstorm in American history swept the land in 1929—stripping individuals and businesses to the bone; plunging men into bankruptcy and out of windows of suicide.

But as the colossal doors opened for America's enforced march into the Depression, there were those who stood firm, refusing to play it cozy until better times returned.

An industrial wedding was proposed, a union between two large flat glass manufacturing organizations— Edward Ford Plate Glass Company and the younger Libbey-Owens Glass Company of Toledo, producers of the only automatic horizontally flat-drawn window or sheet glass in the United States, and limited sizes of plate glass, made by a continuous roll process.

The proposal was made by Ray A. Graham, who with his brothers, Joseph B. and Robert C., had become one of the nation's outstanding firms in industrial investments and management.

Glass manufacture was not new to the Grahams. Back in 1916, the Owens Bottle Company of Toledo had purchased the Graham Glass Company of Indiana, which also controlled Graham Glass of Oklahoma. (The Grahams produced bottles on Graham bottle-blowing machines.)

In the years that followed, the Grahams had organized Graham Truck Corporation, had won high recognition for their management of Dodge Motor Company and had founded Graham-Paige Motors Corporation.

Ray Graham had acquired important holdings in Libbey-Owens Sheet Glass Company through Libbey-Owens Securities Corp., which had purchased the late Edward Drummond Libbey's stock from the trustees of his estate in 1927.

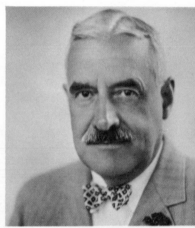

George MacNichol, Jr. He took part in merger negotiations. This photo taken about the time of his marriage in 1922. He had studied at Yale before joining his grandfather's glass business at Rossford.

These and other sales advantages Ray Graham first discussed with George P. MacNichol, Jr., great-grandson of the founder of the American Plate Glass industry, pointing out the improved competitive position a merger could place the two companies in the world of flat glass.

Although Mr. MacNichol, Sales Manager of Edward Ford Plate, had never seen Ray Graham until the day Mr. Graham walked into his office, Mr. MacNichol thought well of the idea and introduced Graham to other Ford executives.

Capt. John B. Ford, the elder, had not selected his favorite grandson to head Michigan Alkali back in the 1880's for sentimental reasons, nor had Edward Ford insisted casually upon a dominant role for his eldest son in the management affairs of Edward Ford Plate Glass years later.

John B. Ford was a good trader. He saw all the potentials Ray Graham visualized. He knew that Edward Ford Plate now ranked high in production facilities. He sensed the effects of the coming Depression, too, and he knew that market promotion sales effort would have to be tremendous to balance the huge sums invested for the new improvements at Rossford.

John B. Ford, Jr.

Mr. Graham, although he wanted to merge, was shaken by the stiff terms insisted upon by Mr. Ford and his associates, but he felt that the Ford price was not excessive when viewed through long-range glasses.

So it was that Ray Graham and one of his associates met in Florida for what was to be an epochal session with John B. Ford, W. W. Knight, vice president and son-in-law of Edward Ford, and George P. MacNichol, Jr., sales manager of Edward Ford Plate, and grandson of Edward Ford.

The merger was approved. Libbey-Owens paid the Ford stockholders 475,000 shares in new Libbey-Owens-Ford . . . admission price to an industrial road show begun 60 years before, without footlights.

Had you been standing in the little park in Ford City, looking up at the majestic bronze likeness of the Father of the American Plate Glass Industry, and had you been able to listen real closely, you would have heard the Old Captain, voice vibrant with triumph, whisper:

"Let's git goin'."

As Chairman of the Board of Libbey-Owens Sheet Glass Company, Mr. Graham visualized the vast potentials of an amalgamation of interests of two flat-glass manufacturing organizations whose products supplemented each other.

Graham could see the strategic ascendancy to a high place in the storefront market with the larger plate glass sheets made by Edward Ford Plate, and for other construction markets, balanced with the promising potential in the new field of automotive laminations (safety glass) then being developed by Libbey-Owens.

THE END

ERECTED IN HONOR OF
JOHN B. FORD
THE FATHER OF THE
PLATE GLASS INDUSTRY
IN AMERICA
BY
THREE THOUSAND EMPLOYEES
ON THE EIGHTIETH ANNIVERSARY
OF HIS BIRTH
NOVEMBER 17, 1891

Statue of Capt. Ford

Bibliography

Material for the first chapter (Highlights of Capt. Ford's career) was obtained from many sources—including records of births, marriages, deaths and wills from dusty files in courthouses of Stanford, Harrodsburg, Frankfort and Louisville, Kentucky.

Personal interviews, notes and advice from the late Calvin Morgan Fackler of Danville, Kentucky, author of "Early Days in Danville"; the late Hattie Scott, Kentucky genealogist; Martha Hieatt, genealogist, Danville; Attorney Jackson D. Guerrant, Danville; J. Winston Coleman, author of many books on Kentucky history, Lexington; Dr. William Newton Craig, Stanford, Kentucky; Dr. Jacqueline Bull, University of Kentucky, Lexington; the late Bayless E. Hardin, and G. Glenn Clift, Kentucky State Historical Society, Frankfort; The Filson Club, Louisville, and many other Kentucky sources.

Records of the Floyd County courthouse, New Albany, Indiana; Attorney John Cody, New Albany; early newspapers and other data in New Albany; New Albany Public Library; many pioneer citizens of New Albany.

Mrs. William Main, Greenville, Indiana, whose father-in-law had been an associate of Capt. Ford; her daughter, Mrs. Ernest A. Smith, Jeffersonville, Indiana; Indiana University library and Indiana State Historical library.

Allegheny court records in Pittsburgh, persons in Ford City and Tarentum, Pa., particularly Dr. F. W. Silsby, who attended Capt. Ford at the time of his death; Arthur Pound's "Salt of the Earth."

Much personal data about Capt. and Edward Ford, along with many of the photographs appearing in this book, were obtained through descendants, including Mrs. Laura Ford MacNichol, Mrs. George Ross Ford, George P. MacNichol, Jr., who has a rare book of clippings on a variety of subjects and kept up by Capt. Ford; Frederick Sloane Ford, John B. Ford, Jr., John B. F. Bacon.

We are grateful to the widow of the late Dr. Elmer Holst, Mary Spencer Hohl, who for many years wrote a newspaper column about Rossford and its citizens, and to Mrs. Lillian Pepper Brown, daughter of the late Matt Pepper for her assistance.

The cooperation of many other Rossfordians is indicated particularly in two chapters of "The Roots Grow Deep," namely "Rossford Personalities" and "The Passing Parade."

Time made it impossible to contact hundreds of Rossfordians whose names should have been recorded in this volume, but we found that the Roots of Rossford indeed grow much too deep for that task. Correct spelling of names and the innumerable dates used were checked and double checked, in the hope that all might be right. If there are mistakes, we are sorry.

The Author
Toledo, 1956.

INDEX OF PERSONALITIES

The following pages carry an index, in alphabetical order, of the names of all individuals, companies and places mentioned in the preceding pages of this book. Following each are the page numbers where mention appears. This index has been compiled as a convenience for readers seeking ready reference to the names of members of their family or friends and other facts. Names of the Ford family are not included due to the repetition of the name throughout the book.